MODERN *Bohemian* CROCHET

UNIQUE CROCHET STITCHES FOR FREE-SPIRITED STYLE

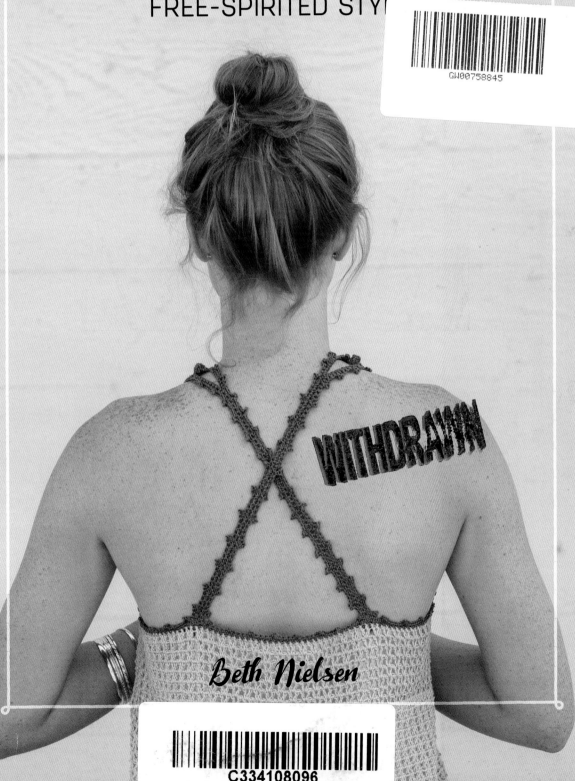

Beth Nielsen

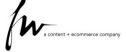

a content + ecommerce company

www.fwcommunity.com

21 20 19 18 17   5 4 3 2 1

Distributed in Canada by Fraser Direct
100 Armstrong Avenue
Georgetown, ON, Canada L7G 5S4
Tel: (905) 877-4411

Distributed in the U.K. and Europe by F&W MEDIA
INTERNATIONAL
Pynes Hill Court, Pynes Hill, Rydon Lane
Exeter, EX2 5AZ, United Kingdom
Tel: (+44) 1392 797680
Email: enquiries@fwmedia.com

SRN: 15CR07
ISBN-13: 978-1-63250-287-2

Editors: Michelle Bredeson and Christine Doyle
Technical Editor: Daniela Nii
Cover and Interior Designer: Michelle Thompson
Illustrator: Daniela Nii
Photographer: Harper Point Photography

Body colorwork chart in Flora Belt adapted from chart
originally published in *Mon Tricot Knitting Dictionary* by Crown
Publishers, Inc., 1972.

Contents

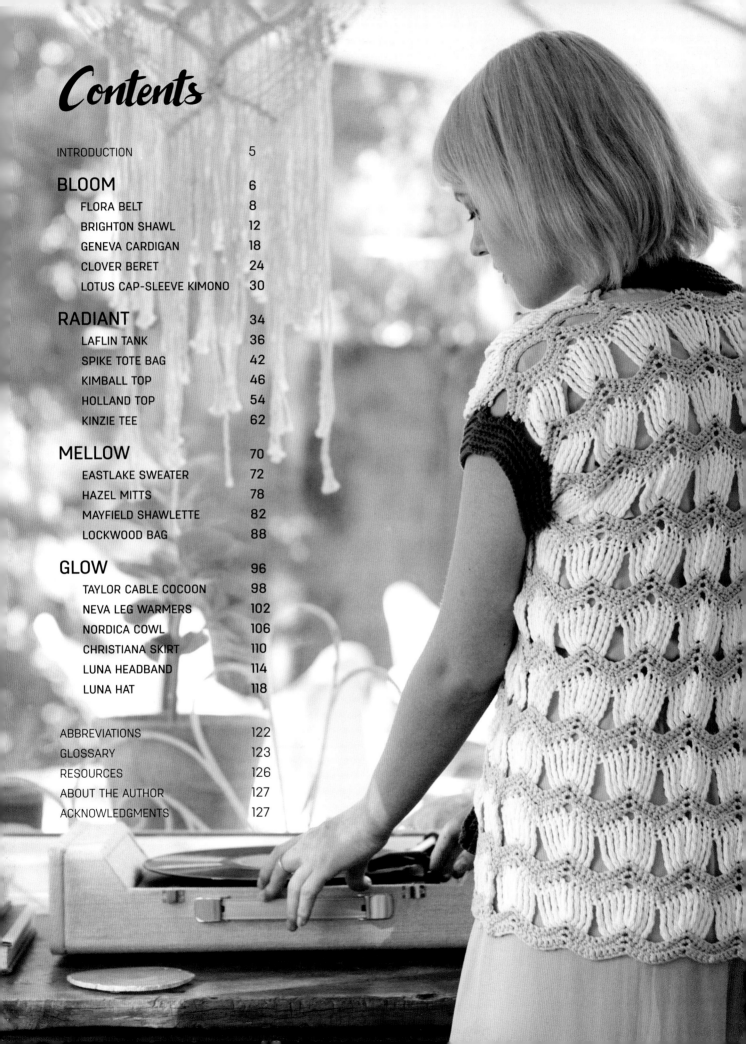

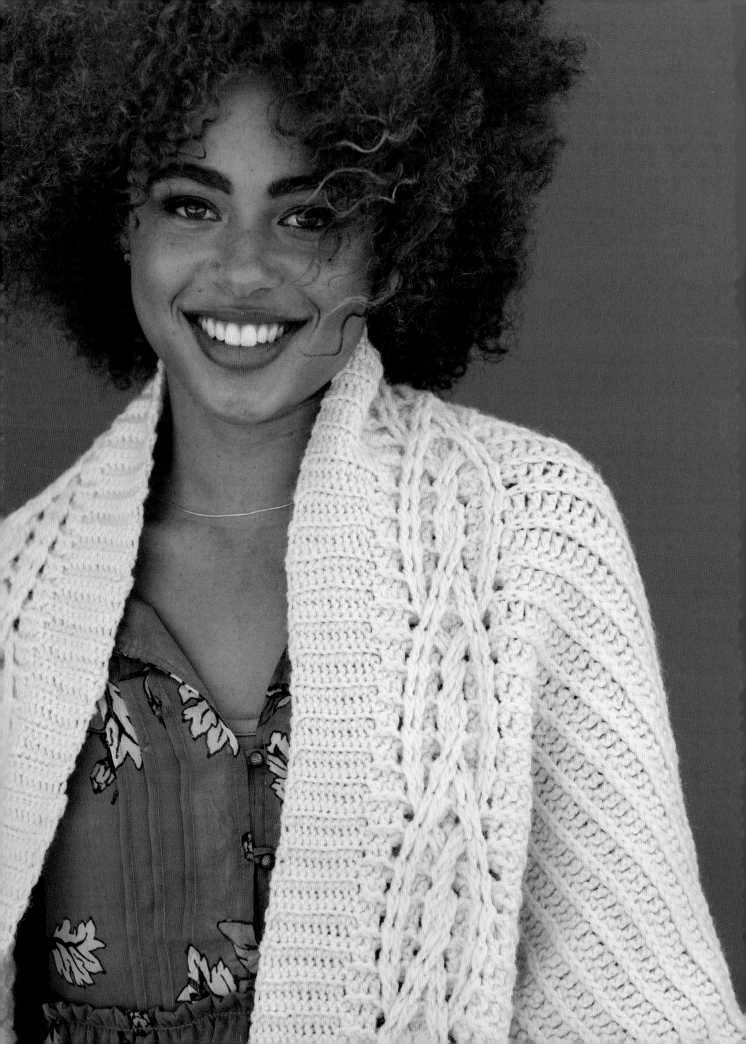

Introduction

When I first taught myself to crochet, I learned how to make a chain. For some reason that was as far as the day's lesson took me, but I was hooked. I made chain after chain after chain until I thought, surely there must be more than this! Once I finally had a small collection of basic skills, I couldn't get enough of the craft. Through the years I learned to knit, which I also love, but there's something about crochet that just keeps drawing me back. I can't keep my hands off a hook for very long without starting to feel the itch. If you're an obsessive crafter like I am, you know exactly what I mean.

As I pursued my love for fashion through college and beyond, I was still drawn to crochet, though as my skills and interest grew I couldn't always find the patterns I was looking for. I wanted modern patterns for the next generation of crafters. Not vintage or retro or throwback, but fresh. New. Innovative.

After I graduated from design school, having been chosen Outstanding Designer in my class, I turned my attention completely to crochet. I was on a mission to create the kind of patterns I was always searching for, and the result is the book you're holding in your hands. I am so honored and thrilled to bring you this collection of patterns that I hope capture a sense of youthfulness, vitality, and exquisite craftsmanship.

If you're a seasoned crocheter, I hope this book brings you a fresh idea or shows you a technique you've never tried. If you're a newbie practicing your chains, I hope these projects keep hooking you in for more!

As you work through these patterns, I want you to keep a few things in mind that I hope will be helpful.

DO WHAT WORKS FOR YOU

I'm over six feet (1.8 m) tall, which makes me a rather unusual size. Every garment pattern I've ever made I've had to adjust and tweak to work for me, and I encourage you to think through what you need and do the same. It's easy to follow a pattern's every instruction, but it's so much more rewarding to complete a garment that's absolutely custom-made for you. So if you need to add (or subtract!) some rows, or change a color, go for it! Make it your own.

DON'T BE AFRAID—TRUST YOURSELF

I want to challenge you to take up a project that seems hard or make an alteration to an existing pattern. The majority of crocheters I've met are absolutely capable of improvising and don't know they are. You can do it! Don't be afraid to make mistakes and don't be afraid to rip out a few rows. Also, if something's not working or doesn't seem right, do what makes sense to you. Don't take my word for it—trust your instincts.

TAKE A STEP BACK

On more than one occasion while making this book, I put my head down to crank some crochet out, and when I stepped back to look at what I'd worked, it was completely wrong. I worked several inches of one project before realizing I was increasing somewhere and then found I had picked up the wrong hook! Keep your eyes open and your mind engaged and you'll save some time and heartache. Step back and look at what you're doing and make sure you're on the right track.

BLOCK IT

I can't stress enough the importance of blocking! I sent a couple projects to a magazine a few years ago without blocking them first, and the next time I saw them (in print!), they were wildly different. That's because when the magazine staff steamed the garments before shooting them, the fibers relaxed and the fabric grew inches. They were way too big and very droopy. It's important to block even your gauge swatches so you know what will happen to the crocheted fabric when it's wet. Blocking gives your projects a professional-looking finish, no matter whether you steam them or completely soak them. It's always worth the time!

Enough talk. Let's get started. I hope you love these patterns!

—Beth

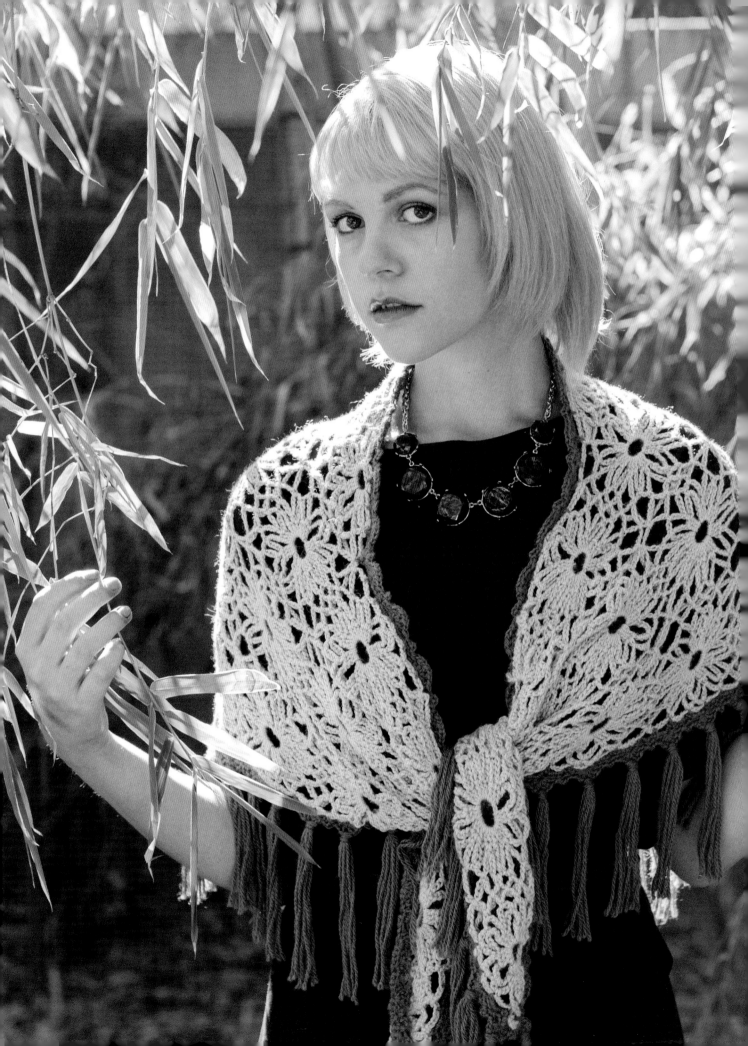

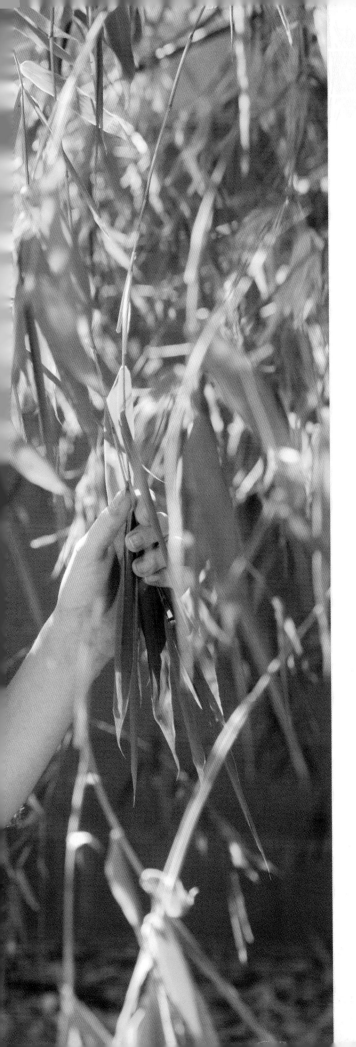

Bloom

When warm breezes blow, soft neutrals set the background for a riot of springtime color. It's time for brightening florals, lighter layers, and silkier yarns with a bit of sheen. These patterns are full of fresh stitches, new techniques, and great style.

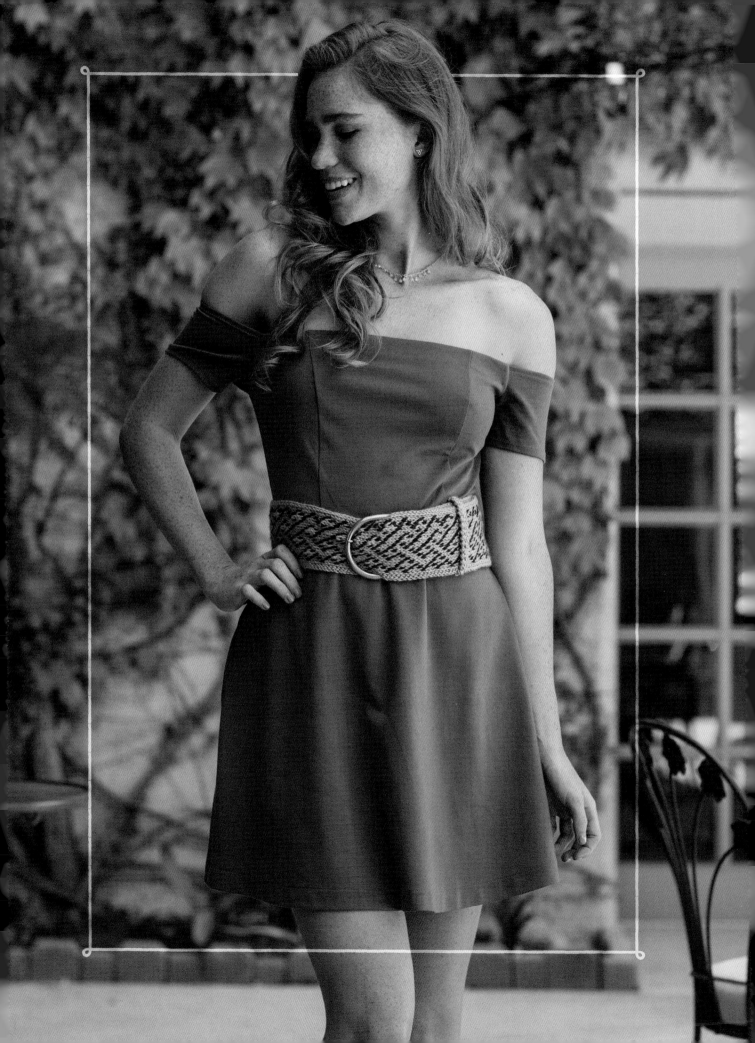

flora belt

Meet your new favorite statement piece. Worked in Tunisian knit stitch, it showcases graphic colorwork. At first glance it almost looks like animal print, but when you look more closely, it becomes an intriguing braided pattern. It might appear to be a knit project, but in Tunisian crochet, it has much more structure and strength. It's shown in three colors here, but it can be made in two colors for simplicity.

FINISHED SIZE
About 3¼" (8.5 cm) wide and 36 (39, 42)" (91.5 [99, 106.5] cm) long.

Belt shown measures 36" (91.5 cm) long.

YARN
DK weight (#3 Light).

Shown here: Patons Silk Bamboo (70% viscose from bamboo, 30% silk; 102 yd [93 m]/2¼ oz [64 g]): #85046 stone (MC), 2 (3, 3) balls; #85310 orchid (A), 1 (2, 2) ball(s); #85607 saffron (B), 1 ball.

HOOK
Size G/6 (4 mm) Tunisian hook.

Adjust hook size if necessary to obtain correct gauge.

NOTIONS
Belt buckle; tapestry needle.

GAUGE
21 sts and 18 rows = 3¼" (8.5 cm) in TKS.

NOTES
Read charts from right to left for all rows, starting at the bottom right corner and working up.

Charts are worked in stranded method. Keep floats loose.

STITCH GUIDE

DECREASE ONE (DEC 1)

Insert hook through 2 sts instead of 1 and draw up a lp—1 st dec'd.

DECREASE TWO (DEC 2)

[Insert hook through next st and draw up a lp] twice (3 lps on hook), yo, draw through all lps on hook—2 sts dec'd.

Belt

With MC, ch 21.

Row 1: FwP: Draw up lp in 2nd ch from hook and in each ch across—21 lps on hook. RetP: Yo, draw through first lp on hook, *yo, draw through next 2 lps; rep from * across. Use this return pass for every row.

Row 2: FwP: TKS in each st across. RetP.

Row 3: FwP: TKS in each st across, working colors according to Row 1 of Body chart. RetP, working lp off the hook with the same color it was worked in.

Cont working in patt through Row 8 of chart, then rep Rows 1–8 until piece measures 34½ (37½, 40½)" (87.5 [95, 103] cm), ending with RetP.

Next row: FwP: TKS in each st across, working colors according to Row 1 of End chart. RetP, working lp off the hook with same color it was worked in.

Dec row: FwP: Working colors according to Row 2 of End chart, dec 1 (see Stitch Guide), TKS in each st across to last 2 sts, dec 1. RetP—2 sts dec'd.

Cont working in patt through Row 10 RetP—3 sts rem.

Last row: FwP: Work dec 2 (see Stitch Guide)—1 st rem. Do not fasten off.

With RS facing, work 9 sc down left side of belt point to smooth out edge. Fasten off.

Finishing

Weave in ends. Steam block. With tapestry needle and using whipstitch, sew buckle to the belt. If your buckle is narrower than the belt (as mine was), simply sc along the top edge, decreasing at the beginning and end of the row until the belt is as wide as the buckle, then sew buckle to the belt.

RING

To create ring that holds belt secure, with MC, ch 30, sl st in first ch to join.

Rnd 1: Ch 1, sc in each ch around, sl st in first sc to join.

Rnd 2: Ch 1, work rsc in each sc around, sl st in first sc to join. Fasten off.

Working along opposite edge, join MC, work rsc in each ch of foundation ch, sl st in first sc to join. Fasten off. Weave in ends.

BODY

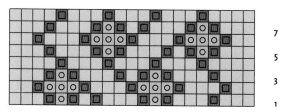

7
5
3
1

21 sts

END

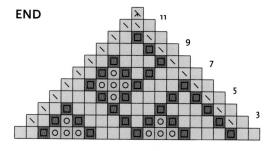

11
9
7
5
3
1

21 sts dec'd to 1 st

STITCH KEY

	with MC, TKS
\	with MC, dec
⋏	with MC, dec 2
▣	with A, TKS
○	with B, TKS

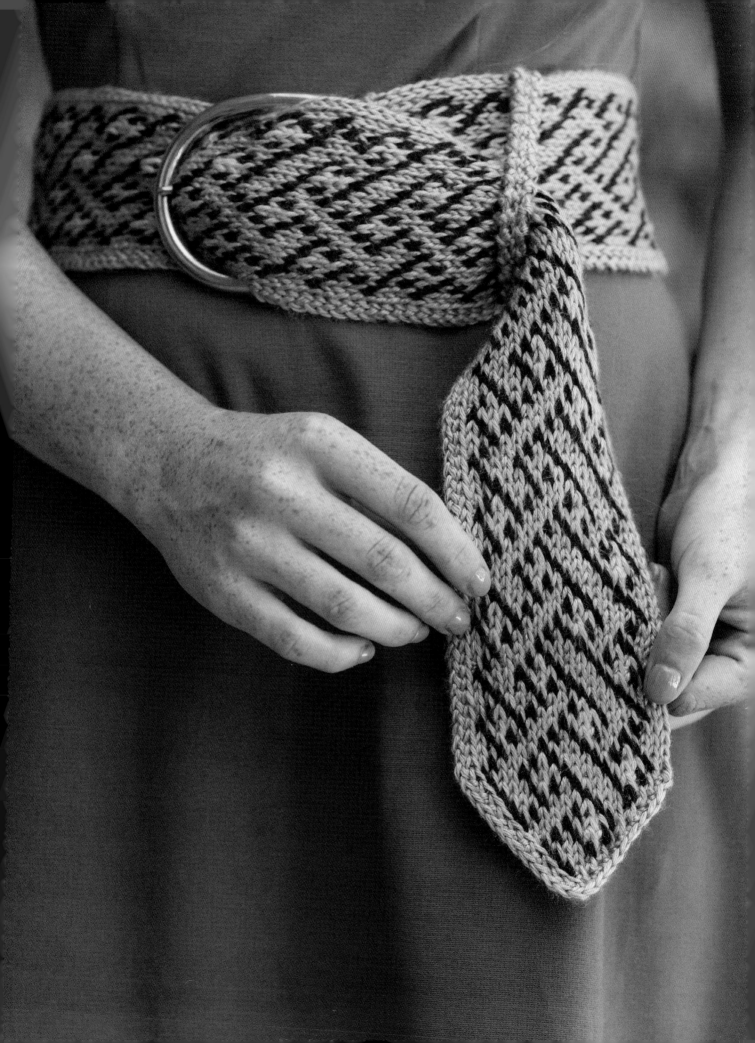

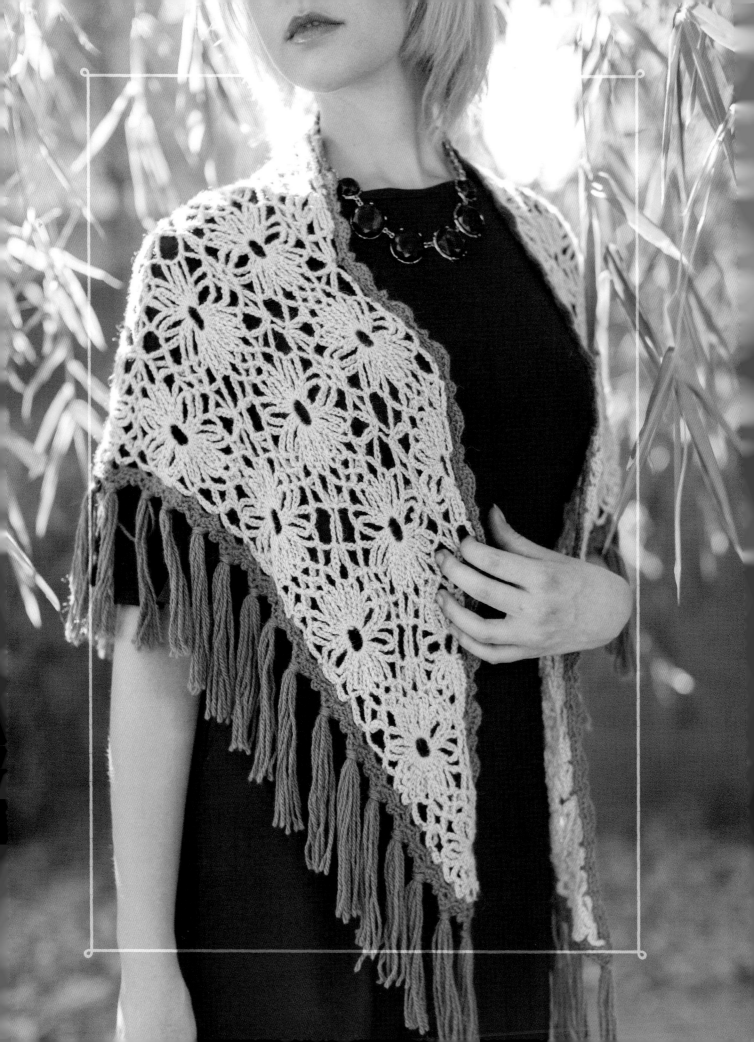

brighton shawl

This airy shawl is perfectly suited for spring with its lacy floral motif. Joining the pieces on the wrong side means you can hardly tell the finished fabric is made of joined motifs; it looks like one continuous whole. Leave the fringe off to keep the shawl more understated and modern, or add it for a classic finish.

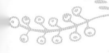

FINISHED SIZE
56" (142 cm) wide and 24" (61 cm) deep, excluding fringe.

YARN
DK weight (#3 Light).

Shown here: Shibui Knits Baby Alpaca (100% baby alpaca; 255 yd [233 m]/3½ oz [100 g]): #2003 ash (MC), 2 skeins; #2002 graphite (CC), 1 skein.

HOOK
Size F/5 (3.75 mm).

Adjust hook size if necessary to obtain correct gauge.

NOTIONS
Tapestry needle.

GAUGE
1 full motif = 4¼" (11 cm).

NOTE
The full motifs are worked in the round with right side always facing, so don't turn at the end of each round. You will turn and work in rows when working the half motifs.

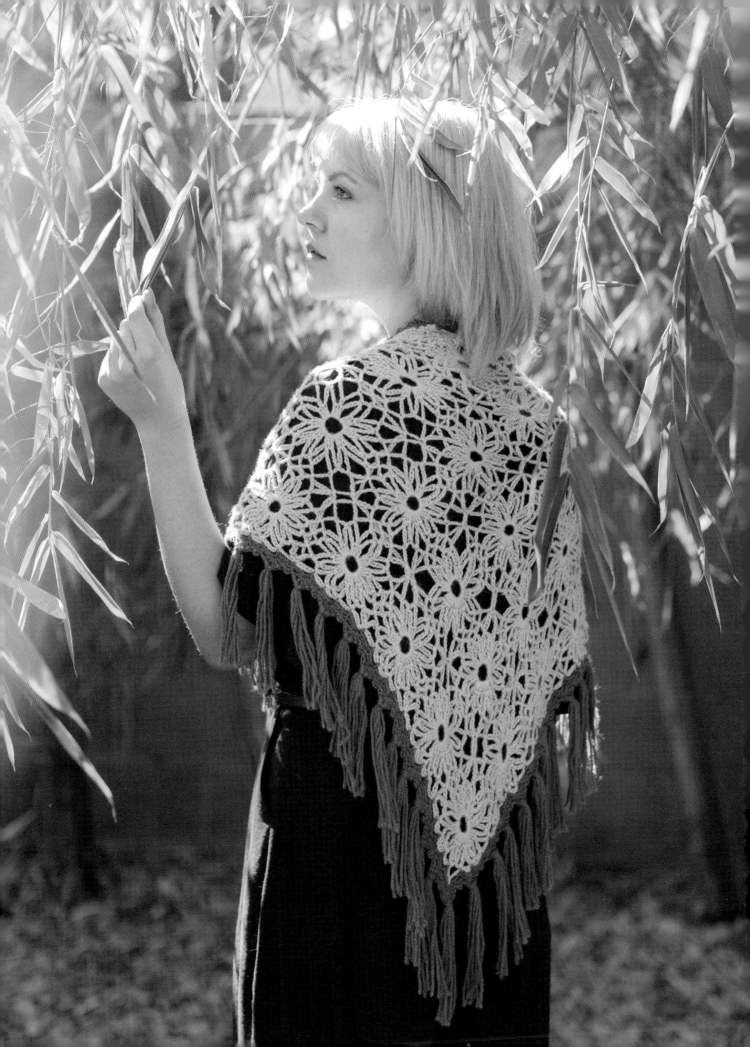

Shawl

FULL MOTIF (MAKE 42)

With MC, ch 10, sl st in first ch to form a ring.

Rnd 1: Ch 3 (counts as dc), 2 dc in ring, [ch 9, 3 dc] 7 times in ring, ch 4, dtr in top of beg ch-3 to join (counts as ch-9 sp)—8 ch-9 sps.

Rnd 2: Ch 1, sc around post of dtr, *ch 6, sk next dc, sc in next dc**, ch 6, sc in next ch-9 sp; rep from * around, ending last rep at **, ch 4, hdc in first sc to join (counts as ch-6 sp)—16 ch-6 sps.

Rnd 3: Ch 1, sc around post of hdc, *[ch 5, sc in next ch-6 sp] twice, ch 11, sc in next ch-6 sp, ch 5**, sc in next ch-6 sp; rep from * around, ending last rep at **, sl st in first sc to join. Fasten off.

HALF MOTIF (MAKE 9)

With MC, ch 10, sl st in first ch to form a ring.

Row 1: Ch 12, [3 dc, ch 9] 3 times in ring, 3 dc in ring, ch 5, ttr in ring, turn.

Row 2: Ch 1, sc in first ch-5, ch 6, [sc in center dc of next 3-dc group, ch 6, sc in next ch-9 sp, ch 6] 3 times, sc in center dc of last 3-dc group, ch 6, sc in ch-12 sp, turn.

Row 3: Ch 11, *[sc in next ch-6 sp, ch 5] 3 times, sc in next ch-6 sp, ch 11; rep from * once, sl st in last sc. Fasten off.

ASSEMBLY

Arrange motifs following assembly diagram. Motifs will be joined on the wrong side. To join motifs, place 2 motifs with right sides together. Working through both thicknesses, join MC and motifs with sl st in any ch-11 corner sp, sc in same sp, ch 6, sc in next ch-5 sp, ch 4, sc in next ch-5 sp, ch 4, sc in next ch-5 sp, ch 6, sc in next corner sp.

ASSEMBLY

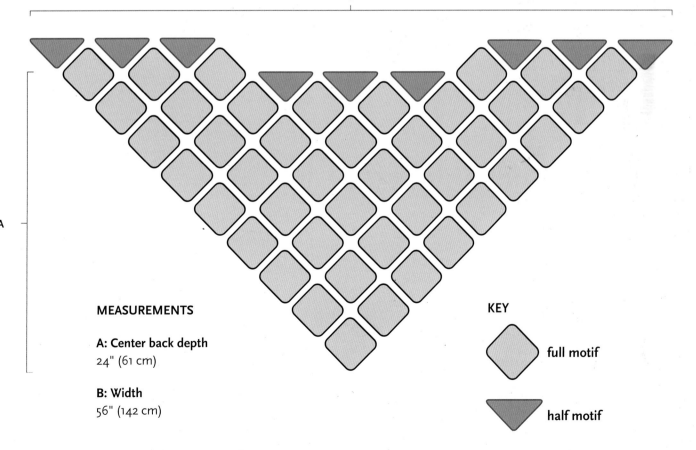

B

A

MEASUREMENTS

A: Center back depth
24" (61 cm)

B: Width
56" (142 cm)

KEY

full motif

half motif

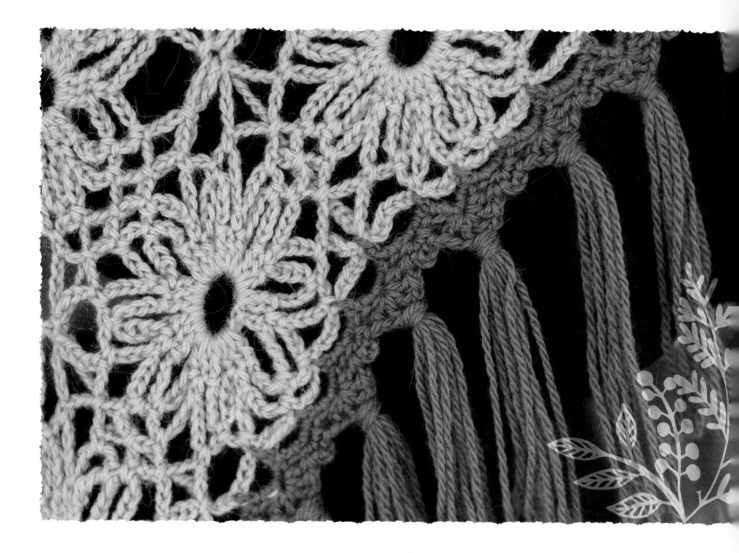

Finishing

EDGING

Join CC in top right corner sp.

Rnd 1: Sc in same sp, *working evenly around edge of shawl, ch 5, sk length so ch-5 is straight, sc in edge of shawl; rep from * around, working 3 sc in each of 3 corners, sl st in first sc to join.

Rnd 2: Ch 1, *4 sc in next ch-5 sp, sk next sc; rep from * around, working 3 sc in each of 3 corners, sl st in first sc to join.

Rnd 3: Ch 1, (sc, ch 3, sc) in first sc, *sk next 3 sc, ([dc, ch 1] 4 times, dc) in next sc, sk next 3 sc, (sc, ch 3, sc) in next sc; rep from * around, adjusting number of skipped sc to end up working ([dc, ch 1] 6 times, dc) in each corner sc, sl st in first sc to join. Fasten off.

BLOCKING

Before adding fringe, wet-block, pin to measurements, and let dry completely. Weave in ends.

FRINGE

For each fringe, cut 5 strands of CC 12" (30.5 cm) each. Hold them together, ends even, and fold in half. Use hook (larger hook may be easier) to pull the lp through point of attachment on shawl. Thread the ends through the lp and pull tight. Put 1 fringe in center of each 5-dc/ch-1 cluster around bottom 2 edges of shawl. Trim fringe to even out strands.

FULL MOTIF

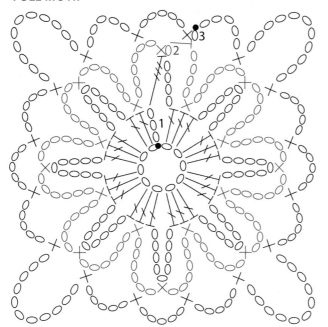

STITCH KEY

- • = slip stitch (sl st)
- ○ = chain (ch)
- ✕ = single crochet (sc)
- Ⱦ = half double crochet (hdc)
- Ⱦ = double crochet (dc)
- Ⱦ = double treble (dtr)
- Ⱦ = triple treble (ttr)

HALF MOTIF

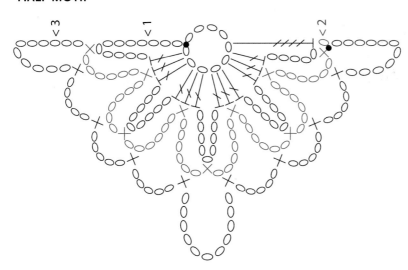

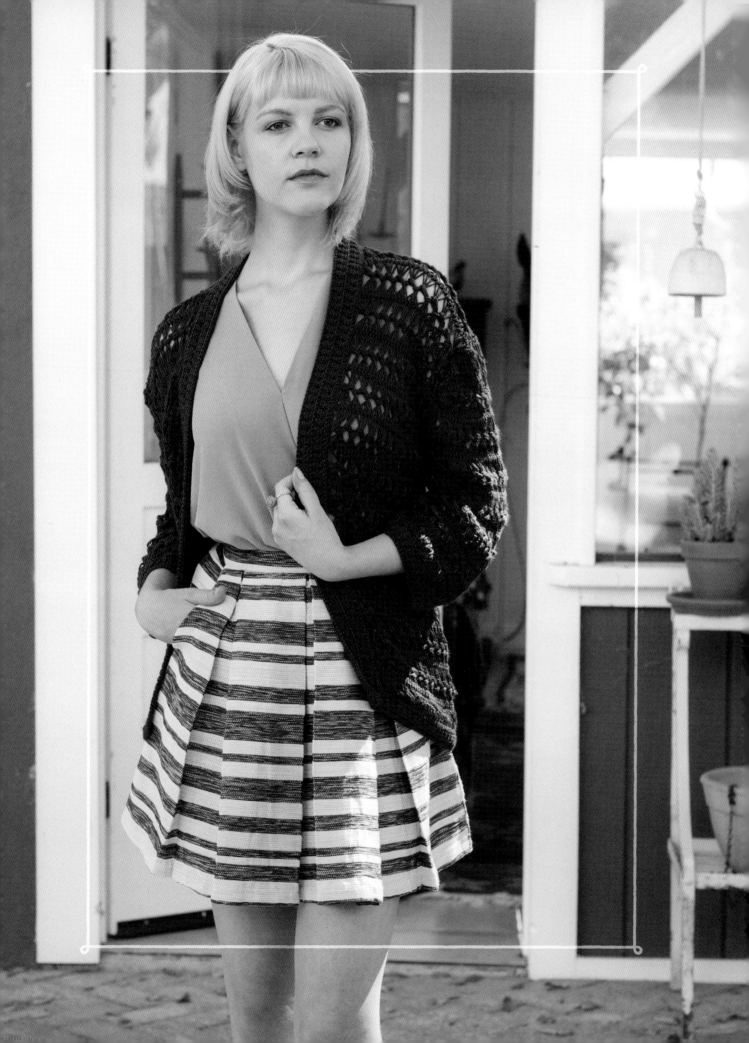

geneva cardigan

This stunning piece uses the hairpin-lace method of crochet to make lovely, delicate lace strips, joined in an unusual way to create an intricate fabric. Hairpin lace looks modern when all the loops are enclosed. Silk-bamboo yarn gives this piece a lovely sheen and light weight.

FINISHED SIZE

About 33¼ (37¼, 41¼, 45¼, 49¼)" (84.5 [94.5, 105, 115, 125] cm) bust circumference, including 1¾" (4.5 cm) wide front bands. Fabric is very stretchy.

Cardigan shown measures 33¼" (84.5 cm).

YARN

DK weight (#3 Light).

Shown here: Patons Silk Bamboo (70% viscose from bamboo, 30% silk; 102 yd [93 m]/2¼ oz [64 g]): #85430 plum, 8 (9, 9, 10, 10) skeins.

HOOK

Size G/6 (4 mm) for hairpin lace; size K/10½ (6.5 mm) for joining lace strips.

Adjust hook size as necessary to obtain correct gauge.

NOTIONST

Hairpin-lace loom; tapestry needle; pins.

GAUGE

Hairpin-lace strip of 21 lps each side = 4" (10 cm) with smaller hook. Prongs of loom are set to 3" (7.5 cm) apart.

NOTES

Hairpin-lace strips are joined from the bottom up. Sleeves are worked separately then sewn.

STITCH GUIDE

TO MAKE HAIRPIN-LACE STRIPS:

Set hairpin-lace loom to 3" (7.5 cm) apart. Remove bottom loom bar, make slipknot with yarn, place lp on left prong, attach loom bar to loom. Wrap yarn around right prong from front to back, hold yarn behind loom, adjusting lp so that slipknot is centered between prongs. Using smaller hook, insert hook under front strand of lp on left prong, yarn over and draw yarn through, ch 1 to secure. *With hook still in lp, flip end of hook from front to back of loom between prongs above yarn, flip loom from the right side toward you to the left so that hook comes to the front, wrapping yarn around loom. Insert hook under front strand of left-hand lp and work a sc; repeat from * until lace strip is the specified length. Slip lps off the bottom of the loom when running out of room.

Determine length of hairpin-lace strip by counting lps along one side. The number of lps made will be double that since there are lps on each side of the center spine.

TO JOIN STRIPS:

Lay 2 strips next to each other flat on a surface, one above the other. Using larger hook, place first 3 lps of top strip on hook. Place first 3 lps of bottom strip on hook and pull through 3 lps of top strip. *Place next 3 lps of top strip on hook and pull through 3 lps of bottom strip. Place next 3 lps of bottom strip on hook and pull through 3 lps of top strip; repeat from * until all lps have been joined.

To keep the join from raveling until edging is worked, use a piece of scrap yarn to tie a bow in the last lp.

TO JOIN A SHORTER STRIP OF LACE TO A LONGER STRIP:

Place the shorter strip above the longer strip with indicated number of excess lps before or after shorter strip and join as follows: work 1 extra lp of bottom longer strip into each 3-lp group of upper shorter strip as many times as indicated (i.e., place 4 lps of bottom strip and pull through 3 lps of top strip).

Body

Make 8 (8, 7, 7, 6) strips with 156 (177, 198, 219, 240) lps each side.

Join strips (see Stitch Guide).

RIGHT FRONT

Note: Place strips so that right strip end matches right front edge.

Make 1 strip with 39 (45, 51, 57, 60) lps each side. Place strip above body and join lps across to last 6 (3, 3, 3, 6) lps of upper strip, then use 4 lower strip lps 2 (1, 1, 1, 2) time(s)—no upper strip lps rem.

Make 1 strip with 33 (36, 42, 48, 51) lps each side. Place strip above last strip and join lps across to last 18 (27, 27, 27, 27) lps of upper strip, then use 4 lower strip lps 6 (9, 9, 9, 9) times—no lps rem.

Make 2 (2, 3, 3, 4) strips with 30 (33, 39, 42, 45) lps each side. Place first strip above last strip and join lps across to last 9 (9, 9, 18, 18) lps of upper strip, then use 4 lower strip lps 3 (3, 3, 6, 6) times—no lps rem.

Join rem strip(s) to previous strip using 3 lps each.

Make 1 strip of 27 (30, 36, 39, 42) lps each side. Place strip above last strip and join lps across to last 9 lps of upper strip, then use 4 lower strip lps 3 times—no lps rem.

BACK

Make 1 strip of 69 (81, 90, 99, 111) lps each side. Place strip above body. Beg with next open lps of body strip after right front, join as foll: use 4 lower strip lps 3 (2, 2, 2, 3) times, then cont with 3 lps across to last 6 lps of upper strip, then use 4 lower strip lps 2 times—no upper strip lps rem.

Make 3 (3, 4, 4, 5) more strips with 63 (75, 84, 93, 105) lps each side. Place first strip above last strip and join as foll: use 4 lower strip lps 3 times, then cont with 3 lps across to last 9 lps of upper strip, then use 4 lower strip lps 3 times—no lps rem.

Join rem strips to previous strip using 3 lps each.

LEFT FRONT

Make 1 strip with 39 (45, 51, 57, 60) lps each side. Place strip above body. Beg with next open lps of body strip after back, join as foll: use 4 lower strip lps 2 (1, 1, 1, 2) time(s), then cont with 3 lps to end—no lps rem.

Make 1 strip with 33 (36, 42, 48, 51) lps each side. Place strip above last strip, join as foll: use 4 lower strip lps 6 (9, 9, 9, 9) times, then cont with 3 lps to end—no lps rem.

Make 2 (2, 3, 3, 4) strips with 30 (33, 39, 42, 45) lps each side. Place first strip above last strip, join as foll: use 4 lower strip lps 3 (3, 3, 6, 6) times, then cont with 3 lps to end— no lps rem.

Join rem strip(s) to previous strip using 3 lps each.

Make 1 strip of 27 (30, 36, 39, 42) lps each side. Place strip above last strip, join as foll: use 4 lower strip lps 3 times, then cont with 3 lps to end—no lps rem.

JOIN SHOULDER

Fold piece with WS tog to match up front top lps with back top lps to be even at armhole edges.

With RS facing, join left front and back using 4 front lps 3 (3, 6, 6, 6) times, then cont with 3 lps from both strips to end of front. Sk next 15 (21, 24, 27, 33) back lps. Join right front and back, beg with next lp of back strip, using 3 lps from both strips across to last 9 (9, 18, 18, 18) lps of back strip, then use 4 front lps 3 (3, 6, 6, 6) times—no lps rem.

Sleeve (Make 2)

Make 4 (4, 3, 3, 3) strips with 75 (81, 96, 105, 114) lps each side. Join the strips.

SHAPE UNDERARM

Make 1 strip of 60 (69, 75, 84, 90) lps each side. Place strip above last strip, join as foll: place 3 bottom strip lps on hook, [place next 3 bottom strip lps on hook and pull through previous 3 lps] 2 (1, 2, 3, 3) time(s), then join strips until no upper lps rem, [place next 3 bottom strip lps on hook and pull through previous 3 lps] 2 (2, 3, 3, 4) times—no lps rem.

SHAPE SLEEVE CAP

Make 1 (1, 2, 2, 3) strip(s) with 48 (57, 63, 72, 78) lps each side. Place strip above last strip, join as foll: use 4 lps of lower strip 6 times, then cont across with 3 lps to last 18 lps of upper strip, then use 4 bottom strip lps 6 times— no lps rem.

Join rem strip(s) to previous strip using 3 lps each.

Make 1 strip of 42 (45, 51, 60, 66) lps each side. Place strip above last strip, join as foll: use 4 lps of lower strip 1 (2, 2, 2, 2) time(s), then cont across with 3 lps to last 9 (18, 18, 18, 18)

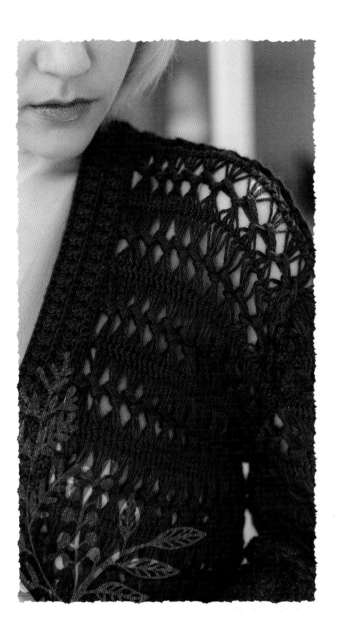

lps of upper strip, then use 4 lps of bottom strip 1 (2, 2, 2, 2) time(s)—no lps rem.

Finishing

SLEEVE EDGING AND SEAM

With smaller hook, join yarn in first lp of bottom strip of lace to work up the sleeve edge. Ch 1, sc in same lp, then *ch 5 to bridge length of lps, sc in center of lace strip, ch 5 to bridge length of lps, sc in both strip-end joined lp groups, locking them in place. Rep from * up one side, around underarm (work 3 sc in underarm corner), up to top of sleeve. Work 1 sc in each lp of top lace strip, then rep from * around and down other side of sleeve. Work 1 sc in each lp at sleeve hem, working 3 sc in corners, sl st in first sc to join. Fasten off, leaving a long tail (about 30" [76 cm] long). Thread tail onto tapestry needle, and using whipstitch, sew sleeve seam. Rep for other sleeve.

ARMHOLE EDGING

With smaller hook, join yarn at base of underarm in lace strip center. *Ch 5 to bridge length of lps, sc in both strip-end joined lp groups, locking them in place, ch 5 to bridge length of lps, sc in center of lace strip; rep from * around entire armhole, sl st in first sc to join. Fasten off, leaving long tail for sewing seam. Thread tail onto tapestry needle, and using whipstitch, sew sleeves into armholes, using pins if necessary to set it in evenly.

SLEEVE HEM EDGING

With smaller hook and WS facing, join yarn in any st along sleeve hem.

Rnd 1: (WS) Ch 1, sc in same st, sc in next 2 sc, *sc2tog in next st, sc in next 3 sc; rep from * around, sl st in first sc to join, turn.

Rnd 2: Ch 1, sc blo in each sc around, sl st in first sc to join, turn.

Rnd 3: Ch 3, dc2tog in first sc, ch 1, sk next sc, *dc3tog in next sc (shell made), ch 1, sk next sc; rep from * around, sl st in top of beg ch-3 to join, turn.

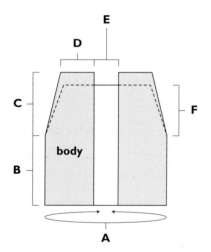

BODY MEASUREMENTS

A: Bust circumference (without band)
29¾ (33¾, 37¾, 41¾, 45¾)" (75.5 [85.5, 96, 106, 116] cm)

B: Bottom edge to underarm
16, (16, 14, 14, 12)" (40.5 [40.5, 35.5, 35.5, 30.5] cm)

C: Upper front height
10 (10, 12, 12, 14)" (25.5 [25.5, 30.5, 30.5, 35.5] cm)

D: Shoulder width
4½ (5¼, 5¾, 6¼, 6¾)" (11.5 [13.5, 14.5, 16, 17] cm)

E: Back neck width
2¾ (4, 4½, 5¼, 6¼)" (7 [10, 11.5, 13.5, 16] cm)

F: Upper back height
8 (8, 10, 10, 12)" (20.5 [20.5, 25.5, 25.5, 30.5] cm)

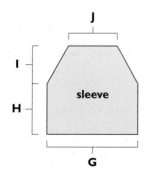

SLEEVE MEASUREMENTS

G: Sleeve width
14¼ (15½, 17¾, 20, 21¾)" (36 [39.5, 45, 51, 55] cm)

H: Sleeve length
8 (8, 6, 6, 6)" (20.5 [20.5, 15, 15, 15] cm)

I: Sleeve cap height
6 (6, 8, 8, 10)" (15 [15, 20.5, 20.5, 25.5] cm)

J: Top sleeve cap width
8 (8½, 9¾, 11½, 12½)" (20.5 [21.5, 25, 29, 31.5] cm)

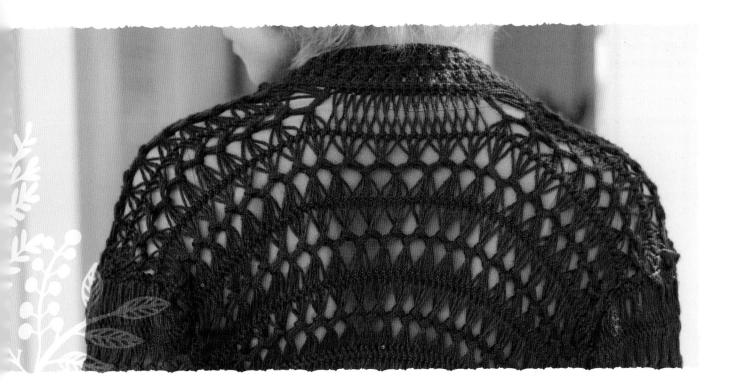

Rnd 4: Ch 1, sc in each shell and ch-1 sp around, sl st in first sc to join, turn.

Rnd 5: Ch 1, sc blo in each sc around, sl st in first sc to join. Fasten off.

Rep for other sleeve.

BODY EDGING

With smaller hook and WS facing, join yarn in first lp of bottom strip of lace to work up the front edge.

Rnd 1: (WS) Working up the front and around the neckline, sc in same lp, then *ch 5 to bridge length of lps, sc in center of lace strip, ch 5 to bridge length of lps, sc in both strip-end joined lp groups, locking them in place. Rep from * up one side to back neck. Work 1 sc in each lp across back neck, then rep from * working down the other side. Work 3 sc in bottom lp at the corner. Work 1 sc in each lp along the bottom of the body. Work 2 more sc in last lp for a total of 3 sc in that corner, sl st in first sc to join, turn. Do not break yarn.

BOTTOM EDGING

Cont to work only across bottom edge.

Row 1: (WS) Ch 1, sc in each sc across bottom edge to next corner, turn.

Row 2: Ch 1, sc blo in each sc across, turn.

Row 3: Ch 3, dc2tog in same st, ch 1, sk next sc, *dc3tog in next sc (shell made), ch 1, sk next sc, rep from * across, turn.

Row 4: Ch 1, sc in each shell and ch-1 sp across, turn.

Row 5: Ch 1, sc blo in each sc across. Do not turn.

FRONT EDGING

Cont to work only along front edges.

Row 1: (WS) Cont with 3 sc in corner, working up front and around neckline, sc in each row-end of hem edging, *sc in next sc, sk next ch, sc in next 4 ch; rep from * up to back neck, sc in each sc across back, then rep from * down other front edge, sc in each row-end of hem edging, 3 sc in corner, turn.

Row 2: Ch 1, sk first sc, sc blo in each sc across, turn.

Rows 3–5: Rep Rows 3–5 of bottom edging, turn.

Row 6: Rep Row 5 of bottom edging, turn.

Rows 7–9: Rep Rows 3–5 of bottom edging. Fasten off.

Weave in ends. If there are wayward lps sticking out of seams, pull them to the WS. Steam block gently, focusing on the collar, hem, and sleeve hems.

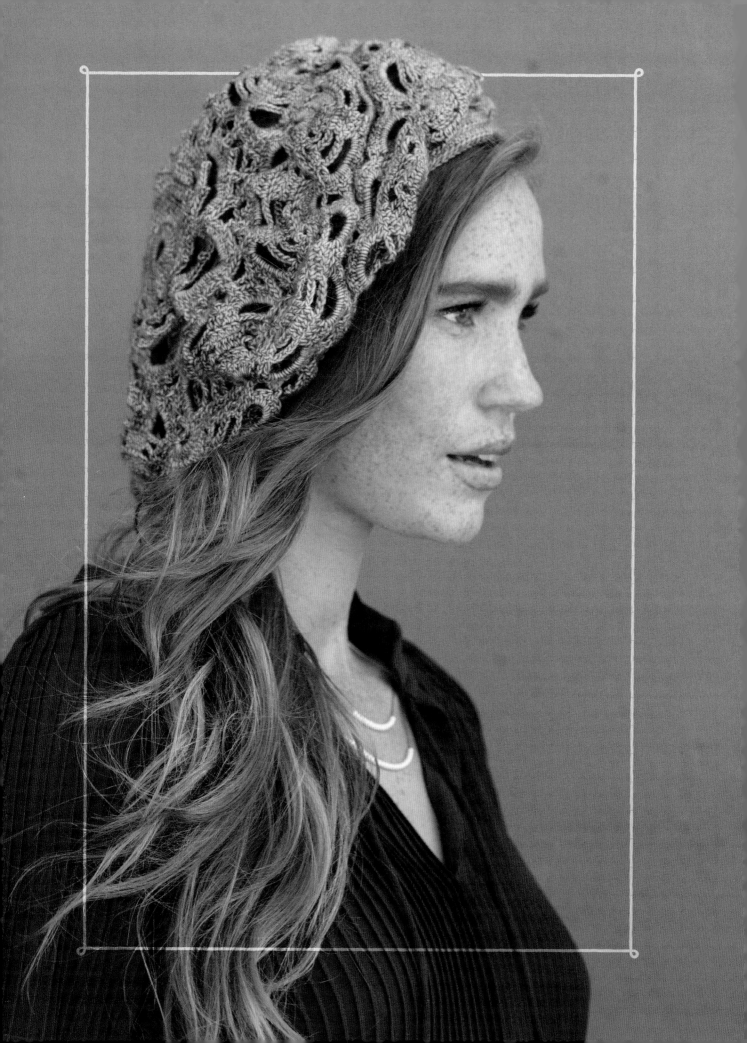

clover beret

This gorgeous topper features a continuous lace design. It looks incredibly complex, but the construction is simple, and the lace pattern is easy to memorize and works up quickly. It's a beautiful showcase for a variegated yarn such as Tosh Merino Light. It'll become an heirloom the moment you finish!

FINISHED SIZE
About 18" (45.5 cm) circumference and 10½" (26.5 cm) diameter. Fits up to 22" (56 cm) head.

YARN
Fingering weight (#1 Super Fine).

Shown here: Madelinetosh Tosh Merino Light (100% superwash merino wool; 420 yd [384 m]/3½ oz [100 g]): filigree, 1 skein.

HOOK
Size C/2 (2.75 mm).

Adjust hook size if necessary to obtain correct gauge.

NOTIONS
Tapestry needle.

GAUGE
Rows 1–6 of first motif make a piece 3½" (9 cm) long and 2" (5 cm) tall, excluding picots.

Lace Strip (Make 2)

MOTIF 1

Ch 8, sl st in first ch to form a ring.

Row 1: Ch 3 (counts as dc throughout), 11 dc in ring, turn—12 dc. Do not join.

Row 2: Ch 3, sk first dc, dc in next dc, [ch 3, dc in next 4 dc] twice, ch 3, dc in last 2 dc, turn.

Row 3: Ch 3, sk first dc, dc in next dc, [ch 4, dc in next 4 dc] twice, ch 4, dc in last 2 dc, turn.

Row 4: Ch 3, sk first dc, dc in next dc, [ch 5, dc in next 4 dc] twice, ch 5, dc in last 2 dc, turn.

Row 5: Ch 3, sk first dc, dc in next dc, [ch 7, dc in next 4 dc] twice, ch 7, dc in last 2 dc, turn.

Row 6: Ch 1, sc in first dc, *(2 dc, picot, [3 dc, picot] twice, 2 dc) in next ch-7 sp, sk next dc**, sc in next 2 dc; rep from * twice, ending last rep at **, sc in last dc. Do not fasten off.

MOTIF 2

Ch 5, turn, dc in sc, turn.

Row 1: Ch 3, 11 dc in next ch-5 sp, sl st in top of first dc of Row 4 of previous motif, turn.

Row 2: Rep Row 2 of Motif 1.

Row 3: Ch 3, sk first dc, dc in next dc, [ch 4, dc in next 4 dc] twice, ch 4, dc in last 2 dc, sl st in top of first dc of Row 2 of previous motif, turn.

Row 4: Rep Row 4 of Motif 1.

Row 5: Ch 3, sk first dc, dc in next dc, [ch 7, dc in next 4 dc] twice, ch 7, dc in last 2 dc, sl st in beg ch-8 ring of previous motif, turn.

Row 6: Rep Row 6 of Motif 1.

MOTIFS 3–14

Rep instructions for Motif 2 twelve times for a strip of 14 motifs. Fasten off.

Center Motif

Ch 8, sl st in first ch to form a ring.

Rnd 1: Ch 3 (counts as dc throughout), 27 dc in ring, sl st in top of beg ch-3 to join—28 dc.

Rnd 2: Ch 3, dc in next 3 dc, *ch 3, dc in next 4 dc; rep from * around, ending with ch 3, sl st in top of beg ch-3 to join—7 ch-3 sps.

Rnd 3: Ch 3, dc in next 3 dc, *ch 5, dc in next 4 dc; rep from * around, ending with ch 5, sl st in top of beg ch-3 to join—7 ch-5 sps.

Rnd 4: Ch 3, dc in next 3 dc, *ch 3, picot, ch 3, dc in next 4 dc; rep from * around, ending with ch 3, picot, ch 3, sl st in top of beg ch-3 to join.

Rnd 5: Ch 3, dc in next 3 dc, *ch 9, dc in next 4 dc; rep from * around, ending with ch 9, sl st in top of beg ch-3 to join—7 ch-9 sps.

Rnd 6: Ch 1, sk first dc, sc in next 2 dc, *sk next dc, (3 dc, picot, [4 dc, picot] twice, 3 dc) in next ch-9 sp**, sk next dc, sc in next 2 dc; rep from * around, ending last rep at **, sl st in first sc to join—7 arches with 3 picot each.

Rnd 7: Ch 3, dc in next sc, *ch 15, dc in next 2 sc; rep from * around, ending with ch 15, sl st in top of beg ch-3 to join—7 ch-15 sps.

Rnd 8: Ch 1, sc in next dc, *(3 dc, picot, [4 dc, picot] 4 times, 3 dc) in next ch-15 sp**, sk next dc, sc in next dc; rep from * around, ending last rep at **, sl st in first sc to join—7 arches with 5 picot each. Fasten off.

Blocking

Before assembly, fully wet-block both lace strips and center motif. No need to pin or stretch the lace, just lay it out and gently press it flat. Let dry completely.

Assembly

Join both lace strips into a circle by sewing or sc together the edges. To join lace strip circles, with WS facing, lay them next to each other with the peaks of the upper piece in the valleys of the lower piece. You will sl st together the picots. There are 9 picots on each motif. Number the picots 1–9 starting from the right and counting left on both pieces. With WS facing, join yarn in any #9 picot of lower piece. *Sl st tog #9 with #1 of next motif of lower piece. Ch 3, sk #5 of upper motif; #5 will always get skipped. Sl st tog #2 of lower motif with #6 of upper motif, ch 3, sl st tog #3 of lower motif with #7 of upper motif, ch 3, sl st tog #4 of lower motif with #8 of upper motif, ch 3, sk #5 of lower motif, sl st tog #9 with #1 of next motif of upper piece, ch 3, sl st tog #6 of lower motif with #2 of upper motif, ch 3, sl st tog #7 of lower motif

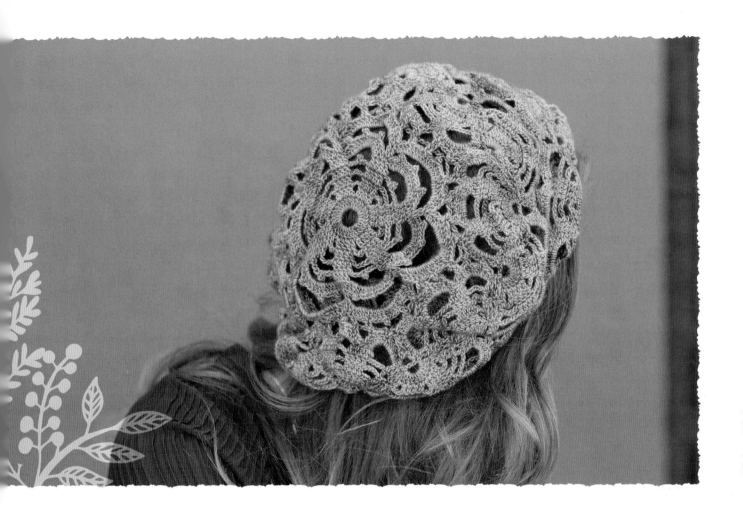

with #3 of upper motif, ch 3, sl st tog #8 of lower motif with #4 of upper motif; rep from * around until strips are joined.

To join center motif, number the picots on each arch 1–5 starting from the right and counting left. With WS facing, place the center motif in the circle made by lace strips with the peaks of the center motif in the valleys of the lace strip. With WS facing, join yarn in any #1 picot of center motif. *Sl st tog #1 of center with #6 of lace motif, ch 3, sl st tog #2 of center with #7 of lace motif, ch 3, sk #3 of center motif, sl st tog #8 with #2 of next lace motif (skipping #9 and #1 of lace motifs), ch 3, sl st tog #4 of center with #3 of lace motif, ch 3, sl st tog #5 of center with #4 of lace motif, sk #5 of lace motif, ch 3; rep from * around until center motif is joined. Fasten off.

Finishing

BAND

With RS facing and lower strip edge at top, number picots again 1–9 from the right to the left. Join yarn in any picot #2 (skipping #1) of lower motif.

Rnd 1: Sc tog #2 with #8 from previous motif (skipping #9), *ch 2, sc in #3, ch 2, sc in #4, ch 2, sc in #5, ch 2, sc in #6, ch 2, sc in #7, ch 2**, sc tog #8 with #2 of next motif; rep from * around, ending last rep at **, sl st in first sc to join.

Rnd 2: Ch 2, hdc in each st around, sl st in first hdc to join.

Rnd 3: Ch 2, hdc in blo of each hdc around, sl st in first hdc to join.

Rnd 4: Ch 1, sc in blo of each hdc around, sl st in first sc to join.

Rnd 5: Ch 2, hdc in blo of each sc around, sl st in first hdc to join.

Rnd 6: Ch 1, sc in blo of each hdc around, sl st in first sc to join. Fasten off.

Weave in ends. Steam block lightly.

Center Motif

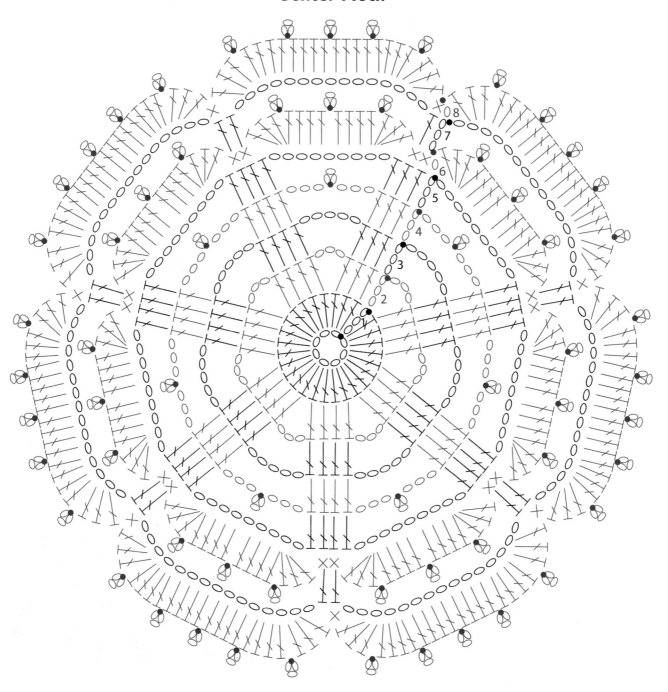

Joining of strips and center

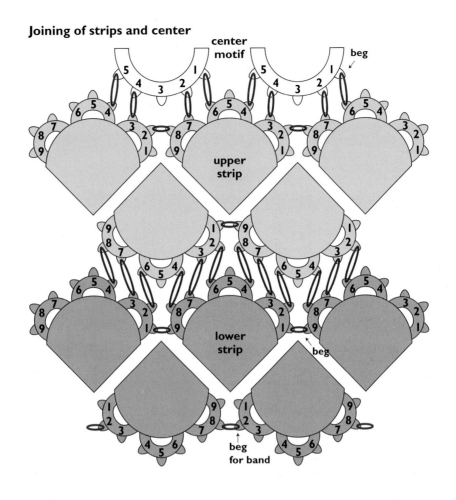

Lace Strip

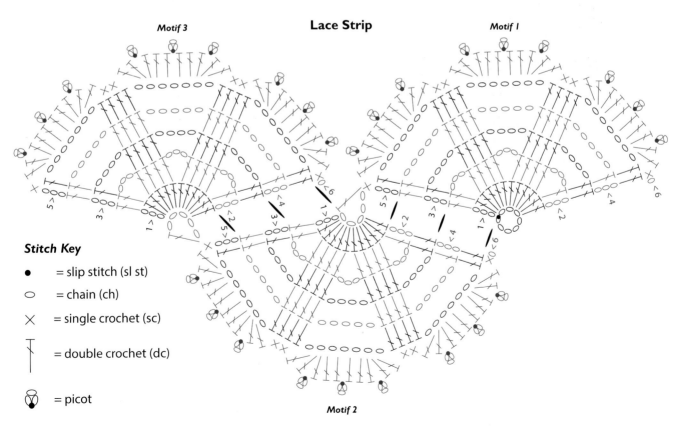

Motif 3

Motif 1

Motif 2

Stitch Key

- ● = slip stitch (sl st)
- ○ = chain (ch)
- ✕ = single crochet (sc)
- ⊤ = double crochet (dc)
- ❂ = picot

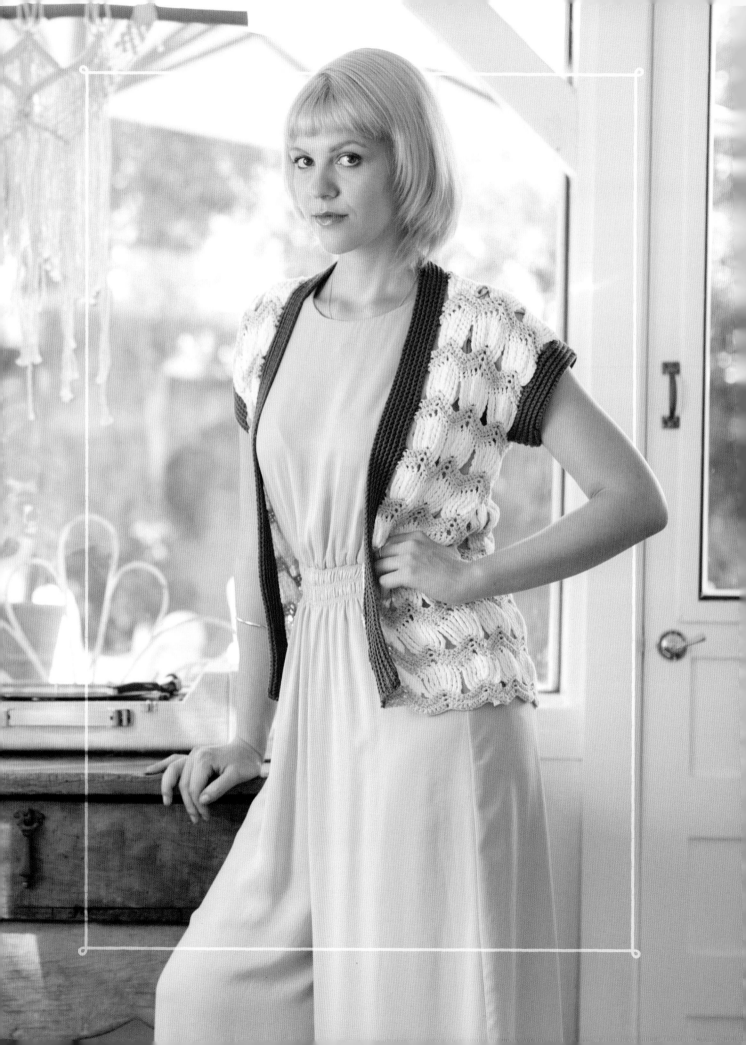

lotus cap-sleeve kimono

I came across this beautiful stitch pattern and knew it would be perfect as an allover texture for a simple garment. I added some bold color contrast and the Lotus Kimono was born. You won't believe how simple the construction of this pattern is. You can spend all your time with the relaxing stitch pattern and not worry about shaping. Different colors would be beautiful here—make it your own!

FINISHED SIZE

About 31 (39, 47, 55, 63)" (79 [99, 119.5, 139.5, 160] cm) bust circumference, including 1½" (3.8 cm) ribbing.

Kimono shown measures 31" (79 cm).

YARN

Worsted weight (#4 Medium).

Shown here: Berroco Modern Cotton (60% pima cotton, 40% modal rayon; 209 yd [191 m]/3½ oz [100 g]): #1603 piper (tan; A), 2 (2, 3, 3, 4) skeins; #1600 bluffs (white; B), 2 (2, 3, 3, 4) skeins; #1630 loon (dark gray; C), 1 (1, 2, 2, 2) skein(s).

HOOK

Size H/8 (5 mm).

Adjust hook size if necessary to obtain correct gauge.

NOTIONS

Tapestry needle.

GAUGE

27 sts (3 fans) and 4 rows (1 rep) = 6" (15 cm) wide and 2½" (6.5 cm) tall in main body patt, blocked.

NOTES

Body is worked in 1 piece from the bottom up to underarms, then fronts and back are worked separately.

All stitches are worked in the back lp only.

Body

With A, ch 127 (163, 199, 235, 271).

Row 1: (WS) Working in back bump of ch, sc in 2nd ch from hook and in next 3 ch, *3 sc in next ch, sc in next 8 ch; rep from * across, ending with sc in last 4 ch, turn—14 (18, 22, 26, 30) 3-sc groups.

Row 2: (RS) Ch 1, sk first sc, *sc in next 4 sc, 3 sc in next sc (center sc of 3-sc group), sc in next 4 sc, sk next 2 sc; rep from * across, turn, leaving last sc unworked—2 sts dec'd.

Row 3: Rep Row 2—122 (158, 194, 230, 266) sts rem. Fasten off.

Row 4 (fans): Sk first 2 sc, join B with sl st in blo of 3rd sc, ch 6 (counts as ttr), ttr in next 2 sc, 3 ttr in next sc (center sc of 3-sc group), ttr in next 3 sc, *sk next 4 sc, ttr in next 3 sc, 3 ttr in next sc, ttr in next 3 sc; rep from * across, turn, leaving last 2 sc unworked—14 (18, 22, 26, 30) fans. Fasten off.

Row 5: Join A with sl st in blo of first ttr, sc in next 3 ttr, *3 sc in next ttr, sc in next 8 ttr; rep from * across, ending with 4 sc, turn—14 (18, 22, 26, 30) 3-sc groups.

Rows 6 and 7: Rep Row 2—122 (158, 194, 230, 266) sts rem. Fasten off.

Rows 8–27 (27, 23, 23, 23): Rep Rows 4–7 five (five, four, four, four) times. Fasten off.

RIGHT FRONT

Row 28 (28, 24, 24, 24): (RS) Sk first 2 sc, join B with sl st in blo of 3rd sc, ch 6 (counts as ttr), ttr in next 2 sc, 3 ttr in next sc (center sc of 3-sc group), ttr in next 3 sc, [sk next 4 sc, ttr in next 3 sc, 3 ttr in next sc, ttr in next 3 sc] 2 (3, 4, 5, 6) times, turn, leaving rem sc unworked—3 (4, 5, 6, 7) fans. Fasten off.

Rows 29 (29, 25, 25, 25)–39: Rep Rows 5–7, then rep Rows 5–7 two (two, three, three, three) more times. Fasten off.

BACK

Row 28 (28, 24, 24, 24): (RS) Join B with sl st in blo of 5th st after end of right front, ch 6 (counts as ttr), ttr in next 2 sc, 3 ttr in next sc (center sc of 3-sc group), ttr in next 3 sc, [sk next 4 sc, ttr in next 3 sc, 3 ttr in next sc, ttr in next 3 sc] 7 (9, 11, 13, 15) times, turn, leaving rem sc unworked—8 (10, 12, 14, 16) fans. Fasten off.

Rows 29 (29, 25, 25, 25)–39: Work as for right front. Fasten off.

LEFT FRONT

Row 28 (28, 24, 24, 24): (RS) Join B with sl st in blo of 5th st after end of back, ch 6 (counts as ttr), ttr in next 2 sc, 3 ttr in next sc (center sc of 3-sc group), ttr in next 3 sc, [sk next 4 sc, ttr in next 3 sc, 3 ttr in next sc, ttr in next 3 sc] 2 (3, 4, 5, 6) times, turn, leaving last 2 sc unworked—3 (4, 5, 6, 7) fans. Fasten off.

Rows 29 (29, 25, 25, 25)–39: Work as for right front. Fasten off.

Finishing

Wet-block piece before continuing.

SHOULDER SEAMS

You will join the chevron peaks of the fronts with the back. With RS facing, join A in 5th sc of front left at armhole edge. *Sc tog this st with its corresponding st on the back. Sc tog next 2 sts, then sl st in next 8 sc of front edge; rep from * until all chevron peaks have been joined. Fasten off. With RS facing, join A in 5th sc of front right at neck edge. Work same as for left shoulder.

COLLAR

With RS facing, join C in bottom right front chevron.

Row 1: (RS) Ch 1, 4 sc in row-ends of first chevron, *ch 6 to bridge next fan, 4 sc in row-ends of next chevron; rep from * 8 more times to right shoulder, ch 10 to bridge shoulder seam, sc in center 3 sc of next chevron peak of back, ch 6, sc in center 3 sc of next chevron peak of back, ch 10 to bridge shoulder seam, **4 sc in row-ends of next chevron, ch 6 to bridge next fan; rep from ** 8 more times, 4 sc in row-ends of last chevron, turn.

Row 2: Ch 1, [sc blo in each sc and ch] across, turn.

Row 3: Ch 1, sc blo in each sc across, turn.

Rows 4–12: Rep Row 3. Fasten off at end of last row.

SLEEVE RIBBING

With RS facing, join C in center of underarm.

Rnd 1: (RS) Ch 1, sc in first 2 sc, *ch 6 to bridge fan, 4 sc in row-ends of next chevron; rep from * around armhole, ending with 2 sc along underarm, sl st in first sc to join, turn.

Rnd 2: Ch 1, [sc blo in each sc and ch] around, sl st in first sc to join, turn.

Rnd 3: Ch 1, sc blo in each sc around, sl st in first sc to join, turn.

Rnds 4–10: Rep Row 3. Fasten off at end of last row.

Weave in ends. Steam block collar and cuffs.

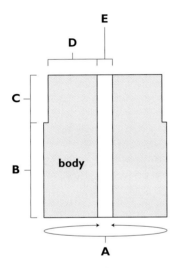

MEASUREMENTS

A: Body circumference without ribbing
28 (36, 44, 52, 60)" (71 [91.5, 112, 132, 152.5] cm)

B: Bottom edge to armhole
15¼ (15¼, 12¾, 12¾, 12¾)" (38.5 [38.5, 32, 32, 32] cm)

C: Armhole height
7½ (7½, 10, 10, 10)" (19 [19, 25.5, 25.5, 25.5] cm)

D: Shoulder width
6 (8, 10, 12, 14)" (15 [20.5, 25.5, 30.5, 35.5] cm)

E: Back neck width
4" (10 cm)

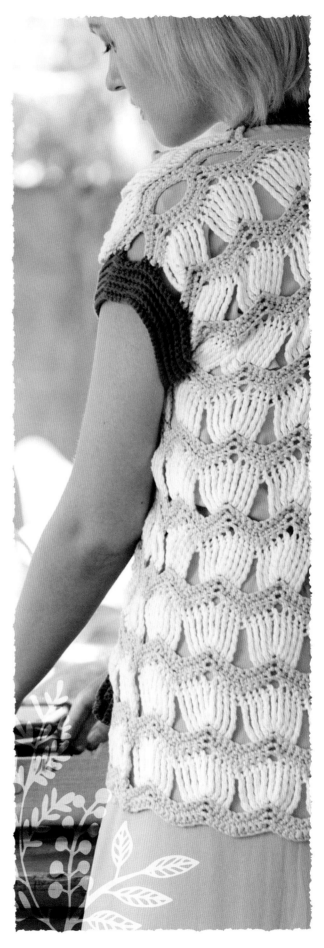

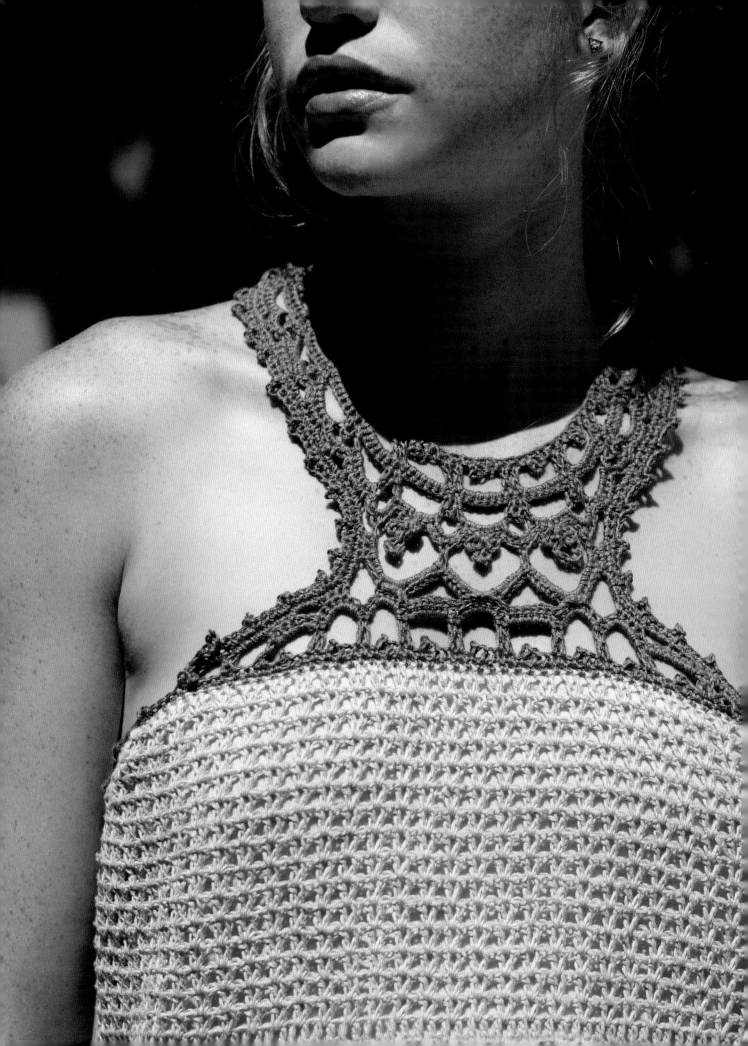

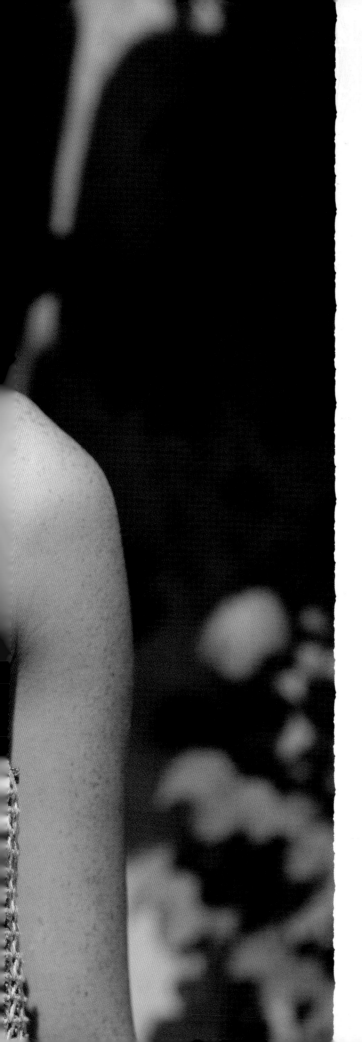

CHAPTER TWO

Radiant

Turn up the heat. Let's get outfitted in bright colors, bold patterns, and statement accessories. Sunny yellows, bright corals, and ocean blues punctuate this collection. These pieces work equally well at a barbecue or over a bikini.

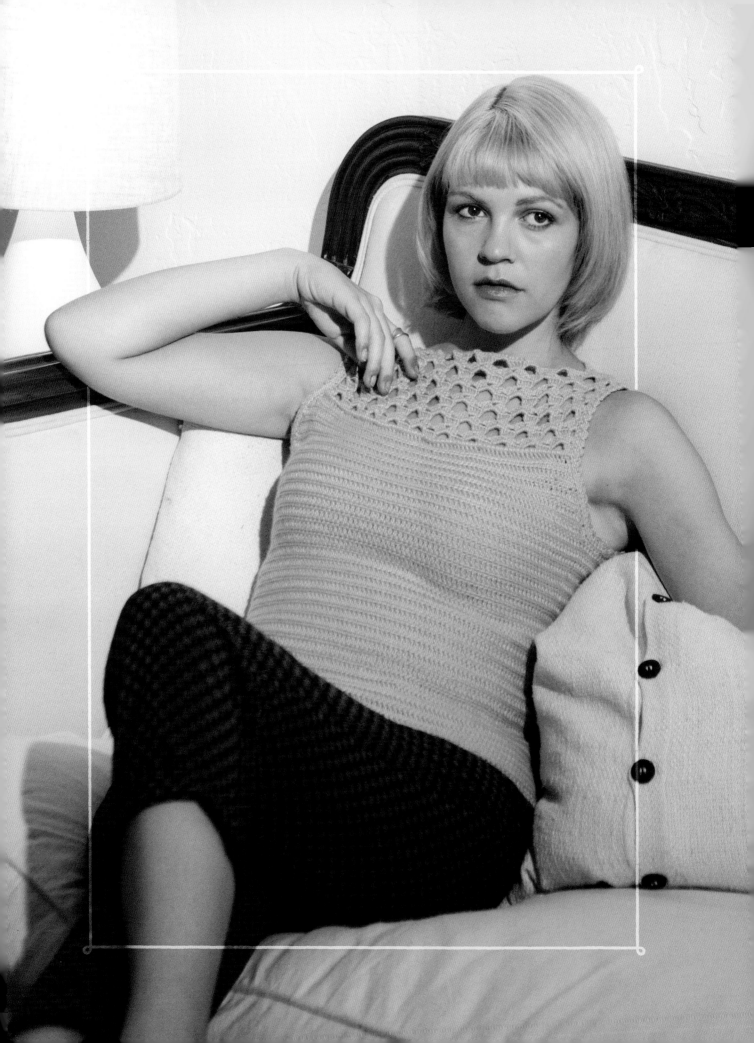

laflin tank

When people talk about crochet being bulky and shapeless, this top is not what they had in mind! This summery tank features a diamond mesh yoke and fits like a glove. The shaping is simple and minimal, and the bateau neckline couldn't be easier. A tiny scalloped edge around the armhole is the perfect finishing detail. Choose a yarn with a light weight and a bit of softness and sheen. Blue Sky Fibers Alpaca Silk works beautifully here.

FINISHED SIZE
29½ (36¼, 40, 44¼, 48)" (75 [92, 101.5, 112.5, 122] cm) bust circumference.

Tank shown measures 29½" (75 cm).

YARN
DK weight (#3 Light).

Shown here: Blue Sky Fibers Alpaca Silk (50% alpaca, 50% silk; 146 yd [133 m]/1¾ oz [50 g]): #144 mango, 6 (6, 7, 7, 8) skeins.

HOOKS
Size G/6 (4 mm) and E/4 (3.5 mm).

Adjust hook size if necessary to obtain correct gauge.

NOTIONS
Tapestry needle.

GAUGE
25 sts and 17 rows in main body patt (alternating rows of sc and dc in the back lp only) = 4" (10 cm) using larger hook.

NOTES
The lower body is worked in the round from the bottom up to the underarms, then front and back are worked with the right side facing at all times to beginning of lacy yoke, fastening off at the end of every row. To avoid weaving in the resulting many tails, work over the tail of the previous row to enclose it.

Tank

RIBBING

With larger hook, ch 6.

Row 1: Sc in 2nd ch from hook and in each ch across, turn—5 sc.

Row 2: Ch 1, sc blo in each sc across, turn.

Rows 3–184 (226, 250, 276, 300): Rep Row 2.

Next row: Sl st along foundation ch to join edges and form a ring. Do not fasten off. Rotate piece to work in row-ends of ribbing.

Body

Rnd 1: (RS) Ch 3 (does not count as dc throughout), dc in each row-end, sl st in top of beg ch-3 to join—184 (226, 250, 276, 300) dc.

Rnd 2: Ch 3, dc blo in each dc around, sl st in top of beg ch-3 to join.

Rnd 3: Ch 1, sc blo in each dc around, sl st in first sc to join.

Rnd 4: Ch 3, dc blo in each sc around, sl st in top of beg ch-3 to join.

Rnds 5–21: Rep Rnds 3 and 4 eight times, then work Rnd 3 once more.

SHAPE WAIST

Place marker (pm) after 92nd (113th, 125th, 138th, 150th) st to mark side seam.

Rnd 22 (dec): Ch 3, dc2tog, dc blo in next 3 sc, dc2tog, dc blo in each sc to 4 sts before m, [dc2tog, dc blo in next 3 sc] twice, dc2tog, dc blo in each sc to last 4 sc, dc2tog, dc blo in last 2 sc, sl st in top of beg ch-3 to join—6 sts dec'd.

Rnd 23: Rep Rnd 3.

Rnds 24–27: Rep Rnds 22 and 23 twice—166 (208, 232, 258, 282) sts rem.

Rnd 28: Rep Rnd 4.

Rnds 29–47: Rep Rnds 3 and 4 nine times, then work Rnd 3 once more.

Rnd 48 (inc): Ch 3, 2 dc blo in first sc, dc blo in next 3 sc, 2 dc blo in next sc, dc blo in each sc to 3 sc before m, [2 dc blo in next sc, dc blo in next 3 sc] twice, 2 dc blo in next sc, dc blo in each sc to last 3 sc, 2 dc blo in next sc, dc blo in last 2 sc, sl st in top of beg ch-3 to join—6 sts inc'd.

Rnd 49: Rep Rnd 3.

Rnds 50–53: Rep Rnds 48 and 49 twice—184 (226, 250, 276, 300) sts.

Rnd 54: Rep Rnd 4.

SIZE 29½" (75 CM) ONLY:

Rnds 55–58: Rep Rnds 3 and 4 twice.

SIZES 36¼ (40)" (92 [101.5] CM) ONLY:

Rnds 55 and 56: Rep Rnds 3 and 4.

ALL SIZES:

There are 92 (113, 125, 138, 150) sts from beg-of-rnd to side marker.

BACK

Begin working as RS rows only (see Notes).

Row 1: (RS) Sl st blo in first 2 (4, 5, 6, 6) dc, sc blo in next 88 (105, 115, 126, 138) dc, sl st blo in next 2 (4, 5, 6, 6) dc, fasten off, leaving rem 92 (113, 125, 138, 150) front sts unworked—88 (105, 115, 126, 138) sc rem for back.

Row 2: (RS) Join yarn with sl st blo in first sc, ch 1, sc blo in same st, hdc blo in next sl st, dc blo in each sc across to last 2 sc, hdc blo in next sc, sc blo in last sc—84 (101, 111, 122, 134) dc rem. Fasten off.

Row 3: Join yarn with sl st blo in top of first dc, sc blo in each dc across. Fasten off.

Row 4: Join yarn with sl st blo in first sc, ch 3 (counts as dc), sk first sc, dc blo in each sc across. Fasten off.

Row 5 (dec): Join yarn with sl st in 3rd dc (remember to count beg ch-3 as a dc), sc blo in each dc across to last 2 dc, fasten off, leaving last 2 sts unworked—4 sts dec'd.

Rows 6–9 (11, 13, 15, 17): Rep Rows 4 and 5 two (three, four, five, six) times—72 (85, 91, 98, 106) sts rem.

Row 10 (12, 14, 16, 18): Join yarn with sl st blo in first sc, ch 3 (counts as dc), sk first sc, dc blo in each sc across to last 2 (1, 1, 1, 1) sc, sc2tog (sc in last st, 2 sc in last st, 2 sc in last st, sc in last st)—71 (85, 92, 99, 106) sts. Do not fasten off after last row.

Row 11 (13, 15, 17, 19): Ch 1, rsc in each st across. Do not fasten off.

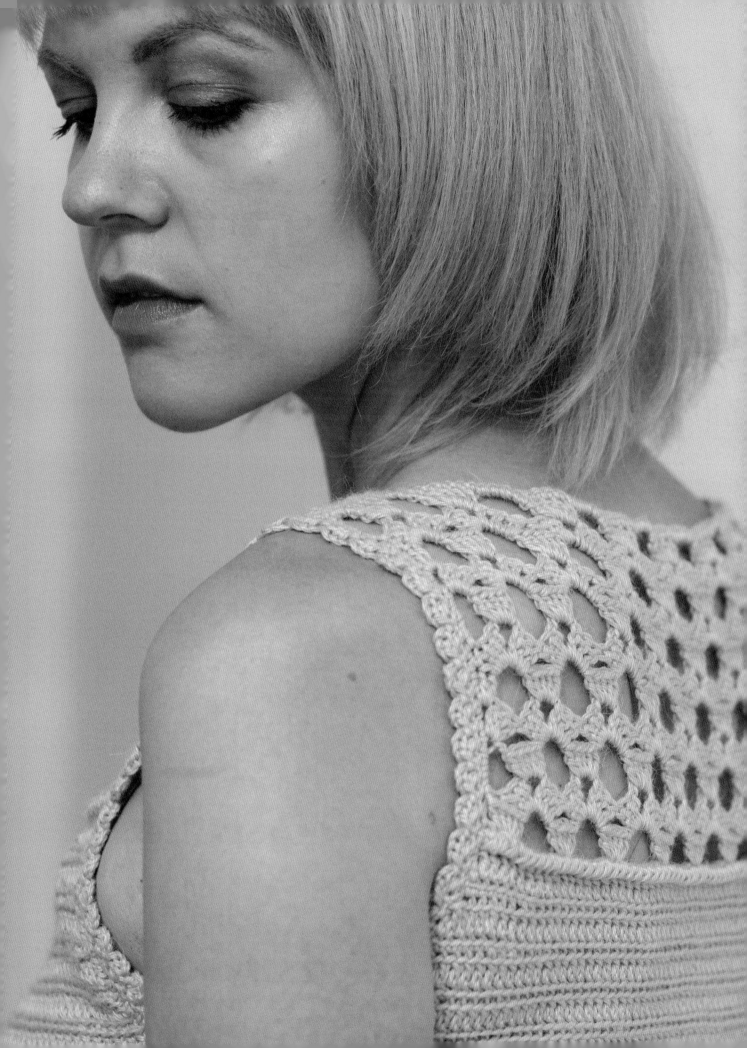

Row 12 (14, 16, 18, 20): Ch 1, BPsc around each rsc across. Fasten off.

YOKE

Change to smaller hook and diamond mesh pattern, working in turned rows.

Row 1: (RS) Join yarn with sl st in first sc, ch 2 (counts as dc), 2 dc in first sc, *ch 4, sk next 6 sc, 5 dc in next sc; rep from * across, ending with 3 dc in last sc, turn—10 (12, 13, 14, 15) ch-4 sps.

Row 2: (WS) Ch 1, sc in first dc, (3 dc, ch 3, 3 dc) in each ch-4 sp across, sc in top of beg ch-2, turn.

Row 3: Ch 5 (counts as tr, ch 1), 5 dc in first ch-3 sp, [ch 4, 5 dc in next ch-3 sp] across, ch 1, tr in last sc, turn.

Row 4: Ch 4, 3 dc in first tr, (3 dc, ch 3, 3 dc) in each ch-4 sp across, (3 dc, ch 1, dc) in beg ch-4 sp, turn.

Row 5: Ch 2, 2 dc in first dc, [ch 4, 5 dc in next ch-3 sp] across, ch 4, 3 dc in beg ch-4, turn.

Rows 6–11: Rep Rows 2–5 once, then work Rows 2 and 3 once more, turn.

Row 12: (WS) Ch 1, work sc in each st and 4 sc in each ch-4 sp across. Fasten off, leaving a 12" (30.5 cm) tail.

FRONT

Begin working as RS rows only (see Notes).

With RS facing, join yarn in last sl st of back at underarm.

Row 1: (RS) Sl st blo in next 2 (4, 5, 6, 6) dc, sc blo in next 88 (105, 115, 126, 138) dc, sl st blo in last 2 (4, 5, 6, 6) dc, fasten off—88 (105, 115, 126, 138) sc rem for front.

Complete front as for back, beg with Row 2 of back.

Finishing

Weave in ends. Steam block lightly.

SEW SHOULDER SEAMS

Thread tail onto tapestry needle, and using whipstitch, sew shoulders for 2 (2½, 3, 3, 3½)" (5 [6.5, 7.5, 7.5, 9] cm), beg at armhole edge and working toward center.

ARMHOLE EDGING

Row 1: With RS facing, join yarn at center of underarm, work an even number of sc around armhole edge, sl st in first sc to join, turn.

Row 2: (WS) Ch 1, sc in each sc around, sl st in first sc to join, turn.

Row 3: (RS) *Sl st in next sc, ch 3, dc in same st, sk next sc; rep from * around, sl st in beg of row to join. Fasten off.

Diamond Mesh

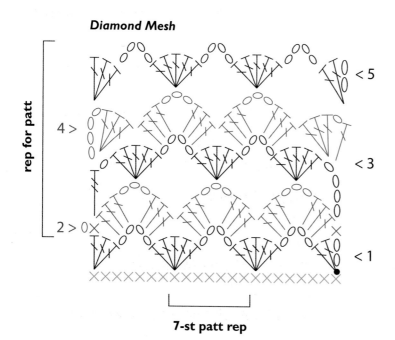

< 5

< 3

rep for patt

4 >

2 > 0

< 1

7-st patt rep

Stitch Key

● = slip stitch (sl st)

○ = chain (ch)

✕ = single crochet (sc)

⊺ = double crochet (dc)

⨎ = treble (tr)

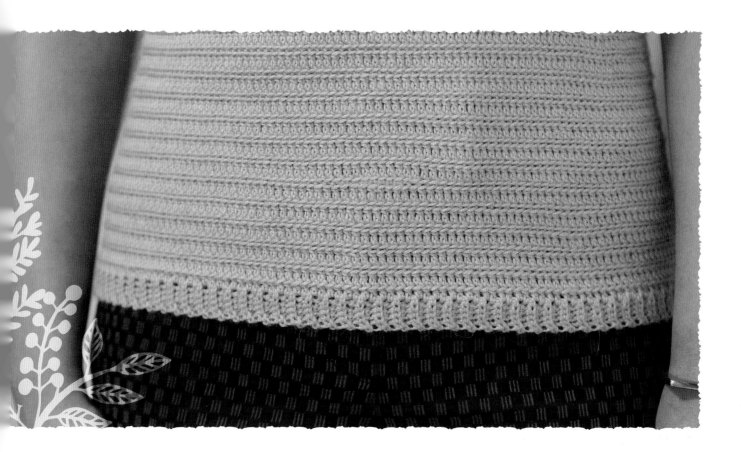

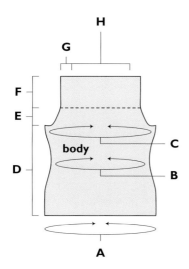

MEASUREMENTS

A: Hip circumference
29½ (36¼, 40, 44¼, 48)" (75 [92, 101.5, 112.5, 122] cm)

B: Waist circumference
26½ (32¼, 37¼, 41¼, 45¼)" (67.5 [82, 94.5, 105, 115] cm)

C: Bust circumference
29½ (36¼, 40, 44¼, 48)" (75 [92, 101.5, 112.5, 122] cm)

D: Bottom edge to underarm
14¾ (14¼, 14¼, 13¾, 13¾)" (37.5 [36, 36, 35, 35] cm)

E: Underarm to beginning of lace yoke
2½ (3, 3½, 4, 4½)" (6.5 [7.5, 9, 10, 11.5] cm)

F: Height of lace yoke
5" (12.5 cm)

G: Shoulder width
2 (2½, 3, 3, 3½)" (5 [6.5, 7.5, 7.5, 9] cm)

H: Neck width
7¼ (8½, 8½, 9½, 9¾)" (18.5 [21.5, 21.5, 24, 25] cm)

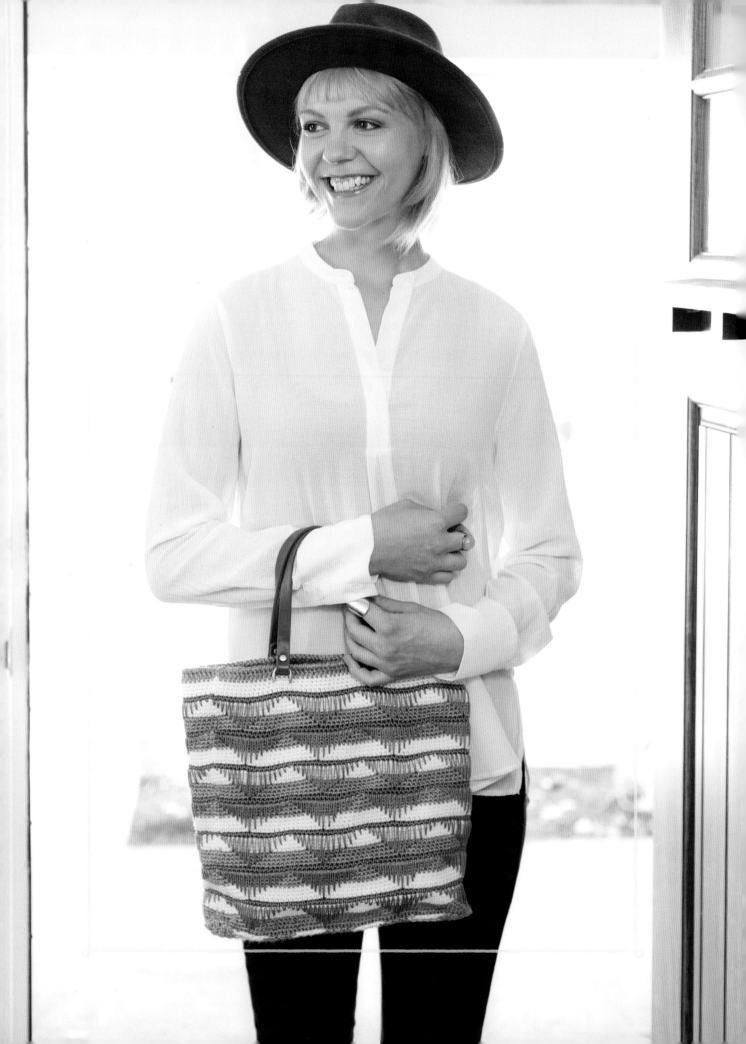

spike tote bag

The simple stripes of this tote are interrupted by bold, contrasting spike stitches in a geometric pattern. This project is inspired by some geometric tapestry crochet projects I came across, but I wanted to see if I could achieve the same effect with spike stitches. The spike stitches are fun to work and make a pattern like you've never seen before! This is one standout accessory.

FINISHED SIZE
About 13" (33 cm) wide and 11" (28 cm) tall.

YARN
Worsted weight (#4 Medium).

Shown here: Caron Simply Soft (100% acrylic; 250 yd [228 m]/5 oz [140 g]): #9509 grey heather (A) and #9701 white (B), 2 skeins each.

Sportweight (#2 Fine).

Shown here: SMC Catania (100% cotton; 137 yd [125 m]/1¾ oz [50 g]): #0252 dark coral (C), 1 skein.

HOOK
Size F/5 (3.75 mm).

Adjust hook size if necessary to obtain correct gauge.

NOTIONS
Stitch markers or straight pins; ½ yd (45.5 cm) fabric for lining (optional); tapestry needle; sewing needle; sewing thread that matches lining; 2 bag handles, 12" (30.5 cm) long.

GAUGE
20 sts and 26 rows = 4" (10 cm) in spike sc patt.

NOTES
This bag is worked with a small hook to ensure a sturdy, dense fabric that can stand up to the spike stitches. If this makes stitching too difficult, feel free to go up a hook size.

Carry the unused colors up the inside of the bag as you go if you're lining the bag. If you choose not to line the bag, fasten off each color after each stripe.

Working sc in the round creates a natural bias. To correct the slant, simply skip the first sc in each row and work the last sc in the skipped st of the previous row. This should realign your seam. You may need to do this every 4 rows or so.

Tote Bag

BASE

With A, ch 11.

Row 1: (WS) Working in back bump of ch, sc in 2nd ch from hook and in each ch across, turn—10 sc.

Row 2 (inc): (RS) Ch 1, 2 sc in first sc, sc in each sc across to last st, 2 sc in last sc, turn—12 sc.

Rows 3 and 4: Rep Row 2—16 sc.

Rows 5–8: Ch 1, sc in each sc across, turn.

Change to B.

Rows 9–16: With B, ch 1, sc in each sc across, turn.

Change to A.

Rows 17–69: Work in sc across, alternating A and B every 8 rows, fastening off at the end of each stripe.

Row 70: Cont with A, ch 1, sc2tog, sc in each sc across to last 2 sts, sc2tog, turn—2 sts dec'd.

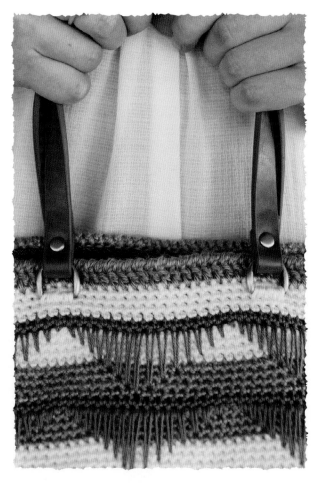

Rows 71 and 72: Rep Row 70—10 sc rem. Do not fasten off or turn after last row.

If using lining, trace around the base onto your lining (no seam allowance needed for base lining if tracing around the outside).

BODY

Continue to work in joined rnds.

Rnd 1: (RS) Cont with A, BPsc around entire edge of base, sl st in first sc to join—164 sc. Do not turn.

Rnd 2: Ch 1, sc in each sc around, sl st in first sc to join.

Rnd 3: Ch 1, *sc in next 6 sc, sc2tog; rep from * around, sc in last 4 sc, sl st in first sc to join—144 sc rem.

Rnd 4: Ch 1, *sc in next 7 sc, sc2tog; rep from * around, sl st in first sc to join—128 sc rem.

Rnd 5: Ch 1, sc in each sc around, sl st in first sc to join.

Change to B.

Rnds 6–9: With B, ch 1, sc in each sc around, sl st in first sc to join.

Change to C.

Rnd 10 (spike row): With C, ch 1, *sc in next sc, sc in next sc 2 rows below, sc in next sc 3 rows below, cont making longer and longer spike sts until you're working in the sc 9 rows below, then shorten spike sts again, working sc 8 rows below, then 7, 6, and so on until you're back up to the previous row, 2 rows below; rep from * around, sl st in first sc to join—eight 16-st spike rep.

It may help to place a stitch marker every 16 sts to help you see where the repeats should be starting and ending. Once this first row of spike sts is established, the rest will be easy. But this first row should be precise so you end up in the right place.

Rnd 11: Rep Rnd 5.

Change to B.

Rnds 12–15: With B, rep Rnd 5.

Change to A.

Rnds 16–19: With A, rep Rnd 5.

Change to C.

Rnds 20 and 21: With C, rep Rnds 10 and 11.

Spike Pattern

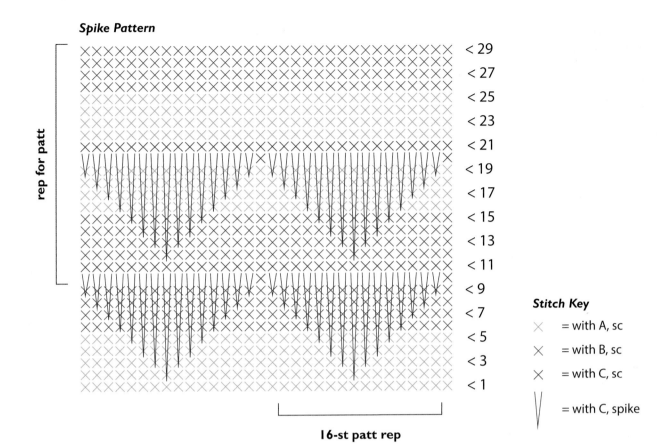

rep for patt

< 29
< 27
< 25
< 23
< 21
< 19
< 17
< 15
< 13
< 11
< 9
< 7
< 5
< 3
< 1

16-st patt rep

Stitch Key

✕ = with A, sc

✕ = with B, sc

✕ = with C, sc

╲╱ = with C, spike

Change to A.

Rnds 22–25: With A, rep Rnd 5.

Change to B.

Rnds 26–29: With B, rep Rnd 5.

Change to C.

Rnds 30–75: Rep Rnds 10–29—6 more spike rows in C.

Change to A.

Rnd 76: With A, ch 2, dc in each sc around, sl st in top of beg ch-2 to join.

Rnd 77: Ch 1, rsc in each st around, sl st in first sc to join. Fasten off.

Finishing

Weave in ends. For lining, measure inner circumference of bag as well as height, adding ½" (1.3 cm) to each measurement. Cut out lining. Fold lining with right sides tog, then sew side seam of lining with a ½" seam allowance, forming a tube. Holding right sides together, sew base of lining to tube with a ¼" (6 mm) seam allowance. Fold top ¾" (2 cm) of lining to wrong side and sew around top about ¼" from top edge. Insert lining into bag, wrong sides together. Using sewing needle and thread, sew lining top edge to below the top of the bag. Using tapestry needle and matching color yarn, sew bag handles to outside of bag about 1" (2.5 cm) below the top edge. Steam block gently.

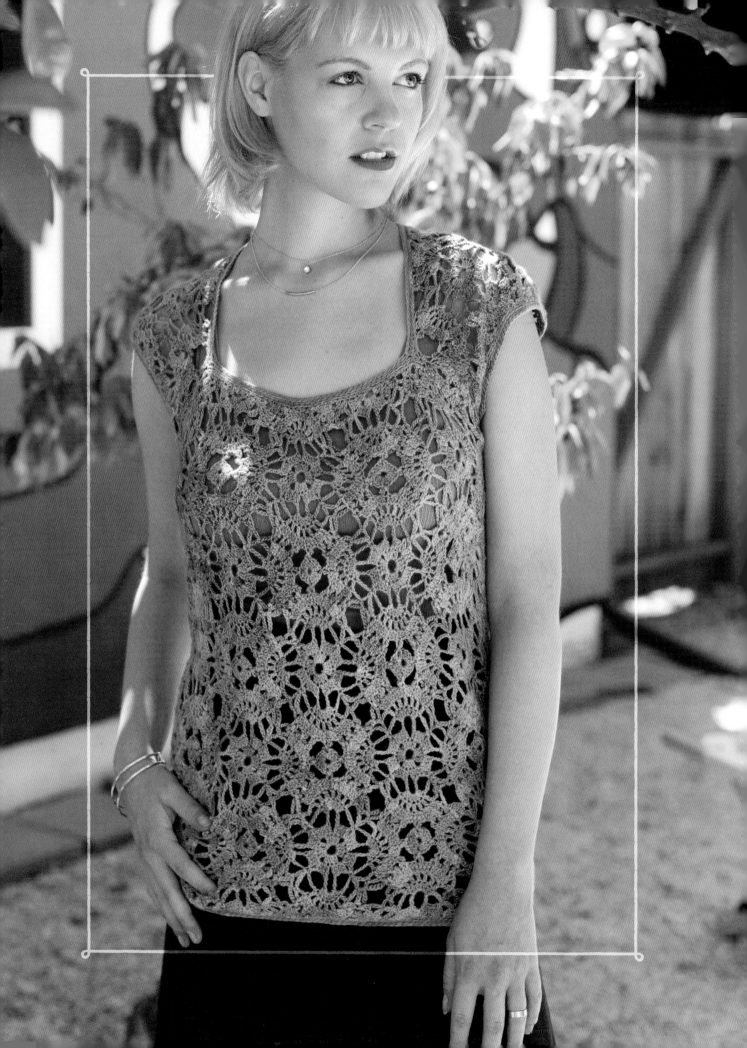

kimball top

One beautiful, repeating motif turns into this easy summer cover-up. With ample length and a relaxed fit, you'll throw this on again and again. The flattering neckline is a simple finish. With its blend of silk and extrafine merino, Manos del Uruguay Fino is a luxurious choice.

FINISHED SIZE
34 (46, 58)" (86.5 [117, 147.5] cm) bust circumference.

Top shown measures 34" (86.5 cm).

YARN
Fingering weight (#1 Super Fine).

Shown here: Manos del Uruguay Fino (30% silk, 70% extrafine merino; 490 yd [450 m]/3½ oz [100 g]): delft, 2 (3, 4) skeins.

HOOK
Size F/5 (3.75 mm).

Adjust hook size if necessary to obtain correct gauge.

NOTIONS
Tapestry needle.

GAUGE
Full motif = 4" (10 cm) square, excluding picots, blocked.

NOTES
The full motifs are worked in the round with right side always facing, so don't turn at the end of each round. You will turn and work in rows when working the partial motifs.

To adjust the length, simply add or remove a row of full motifs.

Top

FULL MOTIF (MAKE 33 [45, 61])

Ch 6, sl st in first ch to form a ring.

Rnd 1: Ch 3 (counts as dc throughout), 3 dc in ring, [ch 2, 4 dc in ring] 3 times, hdc in top of beg ch-3 to join (counts as ch-2 sp).

Rnd 2: Ch 3, dc around post of hdc, dc in next 2 dc, *ch 7, dc in next 2 dc**, (2 dc, ch 2, 2 dc) in next ch-2 sp, dc in next 2 dc; rep from * around, ending last rep at **, 2 dc around post of hdc, hdc in top of beg ch-3 to join (counts as ch-2 sp).

Rnd 3: Ch 1, sc around post of hdc, *ch 4, 7 dc in next ch-7 sp, ch 4**, sc in next ch-2 sp; rep from * around, ending last rep at **, sl st in first sc to join.

Rnd 4: Ch 1, sc in first sc, *ch 6, [dc in next dc, ch 1] 6 times, dc in next dc**, ch 6, sc in next sc; rep from *, ending last rep at **, ch 3, dc in first sc to join (counts as ch-6 sp).

Rnd 5: Ch 1, sc around post of dc, *ch 3, sc in next ch-6 sp, ch 3, [dc in next dc, picot, 2 dc in next ch-1 sp] 6 times, dc in next dc, picot, ch 3**, sc in next ch-6 sp; rep from * around, ending last rep at **, sl st in first sc to join. Fasten off.

HALF MOTIF (MAKE 20 [34, 30])

Ch 6, sl st in first ch to form a ring.

Row 1: Ch 3 (counts as dc throughout), dc in ring, ch 2, 4 dc in ring, ch 2, 2 dc in ring, turn.

Row 2: Ch 3, sk first dc, dc in next 2 dc, (2 dc, ch 2, 2 dc) in next ch-2 sp, dc in next 2 dc, ch 7, dc in next 2 dc, (2 dc, ch 2, 2 dc) in next ch-2 sp, dc in last 2 dc, turn.

Row 3: Ch 3, 2 dc in first dc, ch 4, sc in next ch-2 sp, ch 4, 7 dc in next ch-7 sp, ch 4, sc in next ch-2 sp, ch 4, sk next 2 dc, 3 dc in next dc, turn, leaving last st unworked.

Row 4: Ch 4 (counts as dc, ch 1), sk first dc, dc in next dc, ch 1, dc in next dc, ch 6, sc in next sc, ch 6, [dc in next dc, ch 1] 6 times, dc in next dc, ch 6, sc in next sc, ch 6, [dc in next dc, ch 1] twice, dc in last dc, turn.

Row 5: Ch 3 (counts as dc), picot, [2 dc in next ch-1 sp, dc in next dc, picot] twice, [ch 3, sc in next ch-6 sp] twice, ch 3, [dc in next dc, picot, 2 dc in next ch-1 sp] 6 times, dc in next dc, picot, [ch 3, sc in next ch-6 sp] twice, ch 3, [dc in next dc, picot, 2 dc in next ch-1 sp] twice, dc in last dc, picot. Fasten off.

QUARTER MOTIF (MAKE 8 [0, 8])

Ch 4, sl st in first ch to form a ring.

Row 1: Ch 3 (counts as dc throughout), dc in ring, ch 2, 2 dc in ring, turn.

Row 2: Ch 3, sk first dc, dc in next dc, (2 dc, ch 2, 2 dc) in next ch-2 sp, dc in last 2 dc, turn.

Row 3: Ch 3, 2 dc in first dc, ch 4, sc in next ch-2 sp, ch 4, sk next 2 dc, 3 dc in next dc, turn, leaving last st unworked.

Row 4: Ch 4 (counts as dc, ch 1), sk first dc, dc in next dc, ch 1, dc in next dc, ch 6, sc in next sc, ch 6, [dc in next dc, ch 1] twice, dc in last dc, turn.

Row 5: Ch 3 (counts as dc), picot, [2 dc in next ch-1 sp, dc in next dc, picot] twice, [ch 3, sc in next ch-6 sp] twice, ch 3, [dc in next dc, picot, 2 dc in next ch-1 sp] twice, dc in last dc, picot. Fasten off.

TINY MOTIF (MAKE 29 [45, 57])

Ch 6, sl st in first ch to form a ring.

Rnd 1: Ch 3 (counts as dc), 2 dc in ring, ch 2, [3 dc in ring, ch 2] 3 times, sl st in top of beg ch-3 to join. Fasten off.

Assembly

Arrange motifs following diagram for your size. Motifs will be joined on the wrong side in the picots along the sides, leaving 1 picot open in corner. To join motifs, place 2 motifs with right sides together. Working through both thicknesses, join yarn and motifs with *sl st in first picot after open corner picot, sc in same picot, [ch 3, sc tog next picot] twice, ch 5, sl st in center ch-3 sp of motif closest to you only, ch 5, sc tog next picot, [ch 3, sc tog next picot]. To continue joining around the corner of the motif closest to you, with wrong side still facing, sl st around each post of the 6 dc framing the open 4th corner picot to reach the next picot. Add next motif and join as above.

To join tiny motifs, with wrong side facing, place them in the large holes between the full motifs, sl st the ch-2 sp together with the open picot from the full motif as follows: [ch 3, sl st ch-2 sp and picot tog] until all 4 corners are joined.

When all motifs are joined for front and back, use tapestry needle to whipstitch shoulder seams, beginning at armhole edge and matching up stitches. Whipstitch side seams, starting at the hem and sewing up toward armhole, leaving the last 7 (8, 9)" (18 [20.5, 23] cm) open for the armhole.

Finishing

Weave in ends. Wet-block, pin to measurements, and let dry completely.

NECKLINE EDGING

With RS facing, join yarn in open picot of center motif at back neckline.

Rnd 1: Sc evenly around neck opening, placing sc in picots with ch 1 to next picot or ch 5 to picot of next motif, sc in row-ends of partial motifs adjusting number of sts for even tension, and working sc3tog in the 2 front neck corners, sl st in first sc to join. Do not turn.

Rnd 2: Ch 1, sc blo in same st, sc in each sc and ch around, working sc3tog in corners, sl st in first sc to join.

Rnd 3: Ch 1, sc blo in each sc around, working sc3tog in corners, sl st in first sc to join.

Rnd 4: Rep Row 3. Fasten off.

ARMHOLE EDGING

With RS facing, join yarn at underarm seam.

Rnd 1: Sc evenly around armhole, sl st in first sc to join. Do not turn.

Rnd 2: Ch 1, sc blo in same st, sc blo in each sc around, sl st in first sc to join.

Rnds 3 and 4: Rep Rnd 2. Fasten off.

Rep for other armhole.

HEM EDGING

With RS facing, join yarn at bottom edge at a side seam.

Rnd 1: Sc evenly around hem, sl st in first sc to join. Do not turn.

Rnd 2: Ch 1, sc blo in each sc around, sl st in first sc to join.

Rnds 3 and 4: Rep Rnd 2. Fasten off.

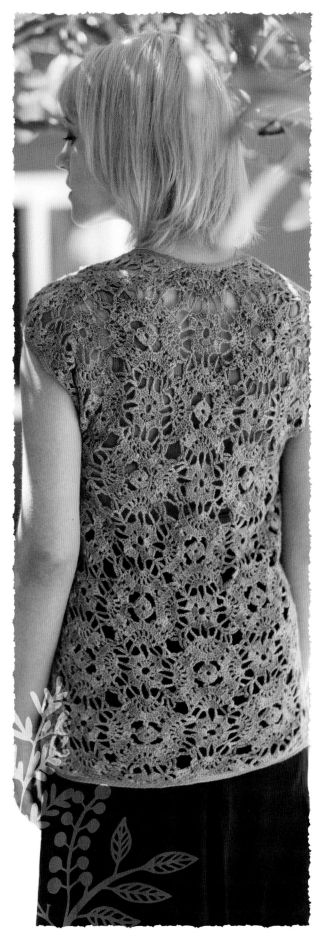

Front, Size 34"

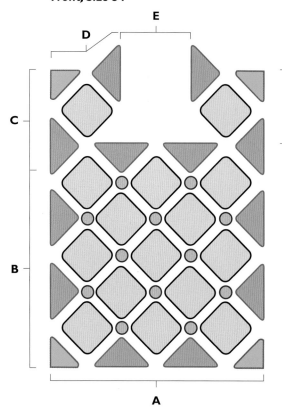

MEASUREMENTS: SIZE 34" (86.5 CM)

A: Width
17" (43 cm)

B: Bottom edge to underarm
18½" (47 cm)

C: Armhole height
7" (18 cm)

D: Shoulder width
6½" (16.5 cm)

E: Back neck width
2" (5 cm)

F: Front neck depth
5" (12.5 cm)

Back, Size 34"

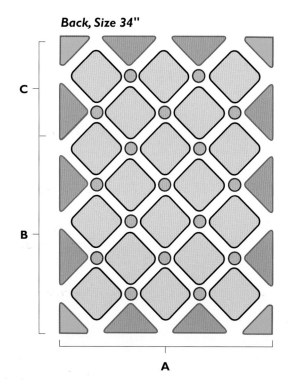

Key

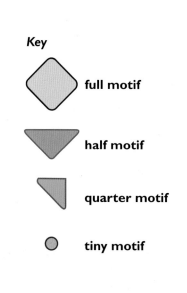

full motif

half motif

quarter motif

tiny motif

Front, Size 46"

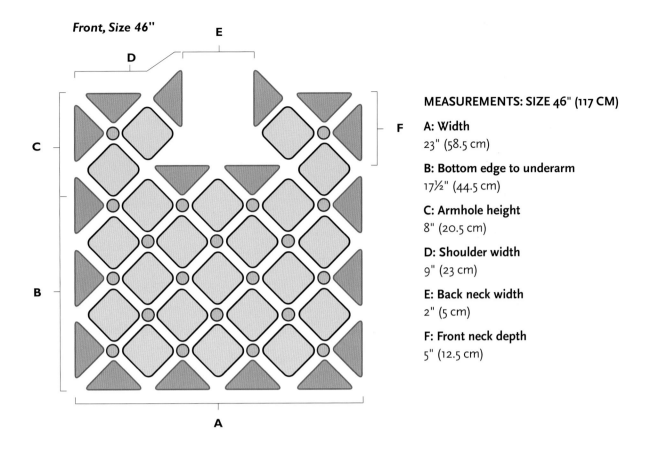

MEASUREMENTS: SIZE 46" (117 CM)

A: Width
23" (58.5 cm)

B: Bottom edge to underarm
17½" (44.5 cm)

C: Armhole height
8" (20.5 cm)

D: Shoulder width
9" (23 cm)

E: Back neck width
2" (5 cm)

F: Front neck depth
5" (12.5 cm)

Back, Size 46"

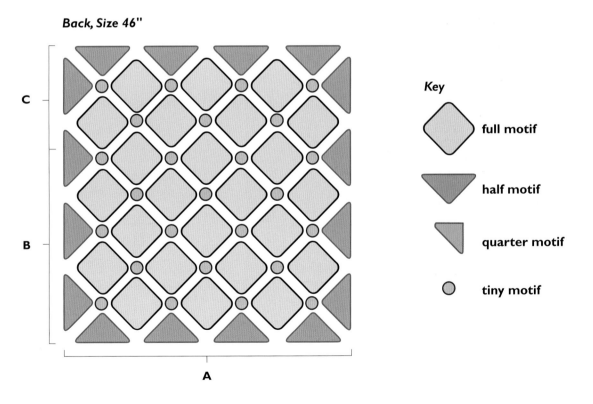

Key

full motif

half motif

quarter motif

tiny motif

Front, Size 58"

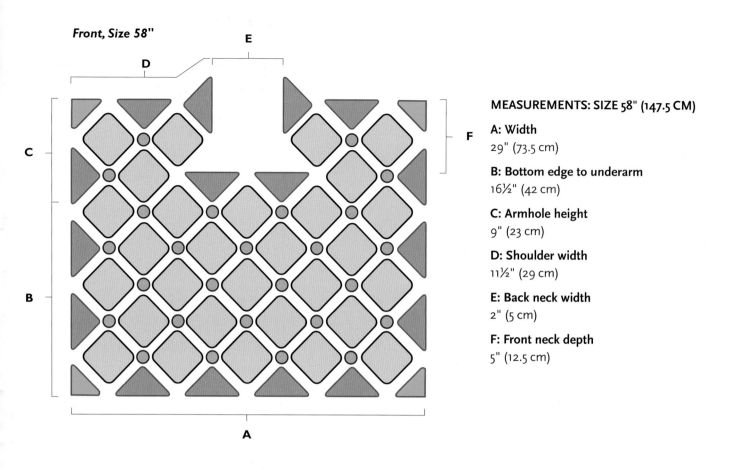

MEASUREMENTS: SIZE 58" (147.5 CM)

A: Width
29" (73.5 cm)

B: Bottom edge to underarm
16½" (42 cm)

C: Armhole height
9" (23 cm)

D: Shoulder width
11½" (29 cm)

E: Back neck width
2" (5 cm)

F: Front neck depth
5" (12.5 cm)

Back, Size 58"

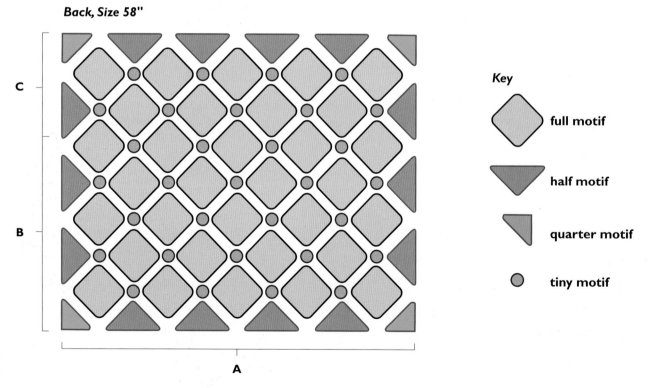

Key

◇ full motif

▼ half motif

◣ quarter motif

● tiny motif

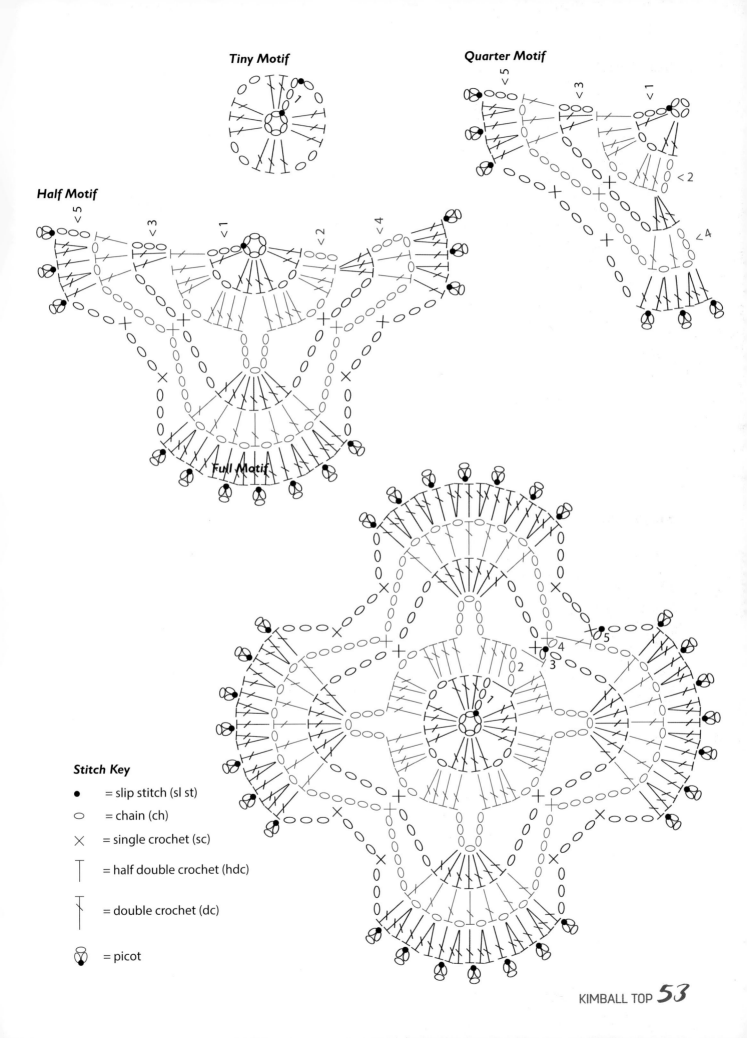

Tiny Motif

Quarter Motif

Half Motif

Full Motif

Stitch Key

- ● = slip stitch (sl st)
- ○ = chain (ch)
- ✕ = single crochet (sc)
- ⊤ = half double crochet (hdc)
- † = double crochet (dc)
- ⊗ = picot

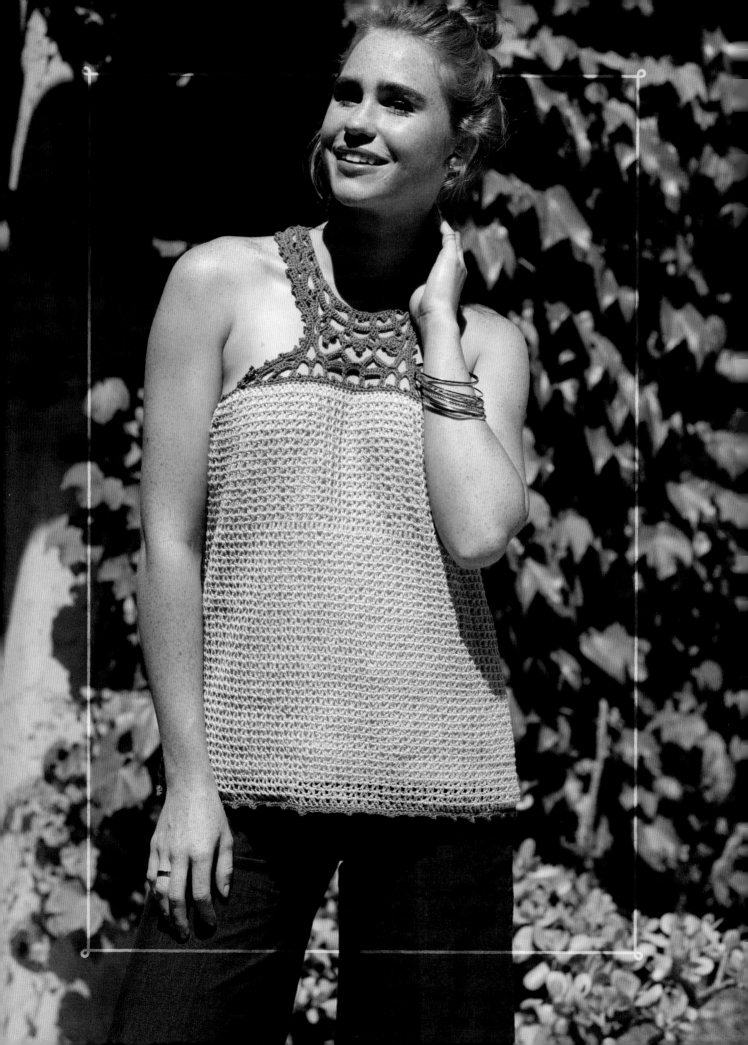

holland top

This top is a showstopper. It's worked in summer-weight linen yarn in a loose, easy silhouette with an intricate, yet not difficult, motif that lies like a bold statement necklace. Wear it unlined as a chic bathing suit cover-up or line it with a lightweight fabric and watch it become your go-to summer staple.

FINISHED SIZE

35 (39, 43, 47, 51)" (89 [99, 109, 119.5, 129.5] cm) bust circumference.

Top shown measures 35" (89 cm).

YARN

Sportweight (#2 Fine).

Shown here: Quince & Co. Sparrow (100% organic linen; 168 yd [155 m]/1¾ oz [50 g]): maize (MC), 4 (5, 5, 6, 6) skeins; paprika (CC), 1 (1, 1, 2, 2) skein(s).

HOOK

Size G/6 (4 mm) and F/5 (3.75 mm).

Adjust hook size if necessary to obtain correct gauge.

NOTIONS

Tapestry needle; ½ (½, ½, ¾, 1) yd (45.5 [45.5, 45.5, 68.5, 91.5] cm) lightweight fabric for lining (optional).

GAUGE

9 v-sts and 11½ rows = 4" (10 cm) in main body patt with larger hook.

NOTES

The body of the top is worked in joined rounds. The upper front will be worked in rows with right side facing all the time.

Foundation ch is at the waistline. You'll work down to the hem, then rejoin at the waistline and work up for the bust.

STITCH GUIDE

V-STITCH (V-ST)

Work 2 dc in same sp. To work a v-st in a v-st, insert hook in bet the 2 dc of a v-st.

QUADRUPLE TREBLE CROCHET (QTR)

Yo 5 times, draw up a lp (7 lps on hook), [yo, draw through 2 lps on hook] 6 times—1 lp rem on hook.

Body

With MC and larger hook, ch 164 (180, 196, 212, 228), sl st in first ch to form a ring, being careful not to twist.

Rnd 1: Ch 3 (counts as 1 leg of first v-st [see Stitch Guide] throughout), dc in 4th ch from hook, sk next ch, *v-st in next ch, sk next ch; rep from * around, sl st in top of beg ch-3 to join—82 (90, 98, 106, 114) v-sts. Do not turn.

Rnd 2: Sl st in first v-st, ch 3, dc in same sp, v-st in each v-st around, sl st in top of beg ch-3 to join.

Rnds 3–7: Rep Rnd 2.

SHAPE WAIST

Place marker in 41st (45th, 49th, 53rd, 57th) v-st for side seam. Move m up as you work.

Rnd 8 (inc): Sl st in first v-st, ch 3, dc in same sp, v-st in each v-st around to m, v-st in sp before marked v-st, v-st in each v-st around, v-st in last sp before first v-st of rnd, sl st in to top of beg ch-3 to join—2 v-sts inc'd.

Rep inc rnd every 8th rnd 3 more times—90 (98, 106, 114, 122) v-sts.

Next rnd: Rep Rnd 2. Fasten off.

BUST

Rotate piece to work in Rnd 1 of body.

Rnd 1 (dec): Join yarn with sl st in first v-st of Rnd 1 of body, ch 3, dc in same sp, v-st in next 39 (43, 47, 51, 55) v-sts, sk next v-st, v-st in each v-st to last v-st, sk last v-st, sl st in top of beg ch-3 to join—80 (88, 96, 104, 112) v-sts rem.

Rnds 2–8: Rep Rnd 2 of body. Do not break yarn.

FRONT

Begin working as RS rows only.

Row 1: (RS) Sl st in first 2 dc, sl st in next v-st, ch 3, dc in same sp, v-st in next 37 (41, 45, 49, 53) v-sts, fasten off, leaving last v-st of front bust unworked—38 (42, 46, 50, 54) v-sts rem.

Row 2: (RS) Join yarn in 2nd v-st, ch 3, dc in same sp, v-st in each v-st across to last v-st, fasten off, leaving last v-st unworked—2 v-sts dec'd.

Rows 3–6 (6, 8, 8, 10): Rep Rnd 2 four (four, four, six, eight) times—28 (32, 32, 36, 36) v-sts rem.

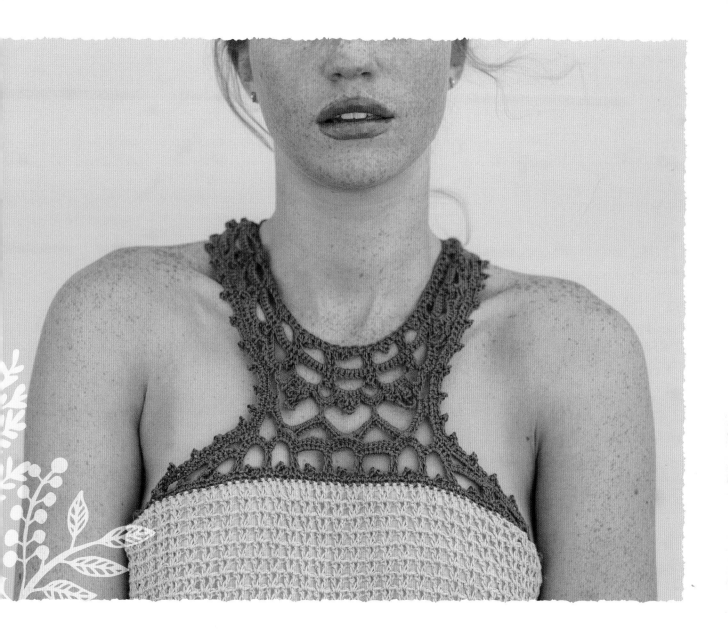

Necklace Piece

With larger hook and CC, ch 46 (54, 54, 62, 62).

Row 1: (WS) Working in back bump of ch, sc in 2nd ch from hook and in next 2 ch, picot, *sc in next 4 ch, picot; rep from * across, sc in last 2 sc, turn—11 (13, 13, 15, 15) picots.

Row 2: (RS) Ch 3 (counts as dc), dc in first sc, *ch 4, sk next (sc, picot, sc), dc in next 2 sc; rep from * across, turn—11 (13, 13, 15, 15) ch-4 sps.

Row 3: Ch 1, *sc in next 2 dc, 6 sc in next ch-4 sp; rep from * across, sc in last dc, sc in top of beg ch-3, turn—90 (106, 106, 122, 122) sc.

Row 4: Ch 1, sc in first 2 sc, ch 6, sk next 6 sc, *sc in next sc, picot, sc in next sc, ch 6, sk next 6 sc; rep from * across, sc in last 2 sc, turn—11 (13, 13, 15, 15) ch-6 sps.

Row 5: Ch 1, sc in first 2 sc, *8 sc in next ch-6 sp**, ch 3, sk next picot; rep from * across, ending last rep at **, sc in last 2 sc, turn.

Row 6: Ch 1, sc in first 2 sc, *sl st in next 8 sc**, 5 sc in next ch-3 sp; rep from * across, ending last rep at **, sc in last 2 sc—11 (13, 13, 15, 15) groups of 8 sl sts. Fasten off.

Row 7: With RS facing, join CC in center of 5th 8-sc group one row below, [(ch 5, sl st, ch 9, sl st, ch 5, sl st) in same sp (large trefoil), sl st across to center of next 8-sc group, (ch 3, sl st, ch 5, sl st, ch 3, sl st) in same sp (small trefoil), sl st across to center of next 8-sc group] 1 (2, 2, 3, 3) time(s), (ch 5, sl st, ch 9, sl st, ch 5, sl st) in same sp (large trefoil), sl st across to center of next 5-sc group, sc in center st of same 5-sc group, turn—2 (3, 3, 4, 4) large trefoils.

Row 8: (WS) Ch 1, sc in first sc, [ch 9, sc in center st of next 5-sc group] 3 (3, 5, 5, 7) times, turn—3 (5, 5, 7, 7) ch-9 sps.

Row 9: (RS) Ch 1, 17 sc in each ch-9 sp across—3 (5, 5, 7, 7) groups of 17 sc. Fasten off.

Finishing

BODY EDGING

With RS facing and larger hook, join CC in first unworked dc at end of Row 1 of front (right underarm).

Rnd 1: (RS) Ch 1, sc in same sp, sc in each dc around back to opposite underarm, when you get to bust rows, [sc in top of next beg ch-3, sc in next dc] 6 (6, 8, 8, 10) times to top of bustline, sc in each dc across top of bustline, sc in next 10 (10, 14, 14, 18) dc down edge of bustline rows, sl st to first sc to join. Do not turn—160 (176, 192, 208, 224) sc.

Rnd 2: (RS) Ch 1, sc in same sp, sc in next 3 sc, picot, *sc in next 4 sc, picot; rep from * around, sl st in first sc to join—40 (44, 48, 52, 56) picots. Fasten off.

Locate center 9 (13, 13, 17, 17) picots of the front bustline. With RS facing, join CC in 3rd sc to the right of the first center picot.

Row 3: (RS) Ch 3 (counts as dc), dc in next sc, [ch 4, sk next (sc, picot, sc), dc in next 2 sc] 9 (13, 13, 17, 17) times, turn—9 (13, 13, 17, 17) ch-4 sps.

Row 4: (WS) Ch 1, [sk next 2 dc, 7 sc in next ch-4 sp] across, sl st in top of beg ch-3. Fasten off.

ASSEMBLY

To join the necklace piece to the body, with RS facing, lay both pieces next to each other on a flat surface, arches of necklace centered over arches of body edging. With smaller hook, join CC in 3rd sc of 3rd 7-sc arch of body edging from the right. *Sl st tog center 3 sc from arch of body with arch of necklace piece, sl st across rem sc of current arch and next arch of body, sl st in first 2 sc of next arch of body; rep from * until all arches of necklace piece have been joined. There will be 2 unused body arches on each side of joined arches. Fasten off.

EDGING/STRAPS

With right side facing and smaller hook, join CC in 2nd picot to the right of first arch of body edging.

Row 1: (RS) Sc in same sp, ch 3, sc in next picot, ch 3, sc in center 3 sc of first arch, ch 3, sc in center 3 sc of next arch, ch 3, sc in beg 3 sc of first arch of necklace, cont to work along necklace piece, ch 3, *sc in 3rd, 4th, and 5th sc of next

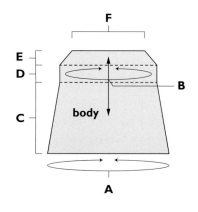

MEASUREMENTS

A: Hip circumference
40 (43½, 47¼, 50¾, 54¼)" (101.5 [110.5, 120, 129, 138] cm)

B: Bust circumference
35½ (39¼, 42¾, 46¼, 49¾)" (90 [99.5, 108.5, 117.5, 126.5] cm)

C: Body length worked downward
11½" (29 cm)

D: Waist to underarm worked upward
2¾" (7 cm)

E: Front height from underarm to top
2 (2, 2¾, 2¾, 3½)" (5 [5, 7, 7, 9] cm)

F: Front top width
12½ (14¼, 14¼, 16, 16)" (31.5 [36, 36, 40.5, 40.5] cm)

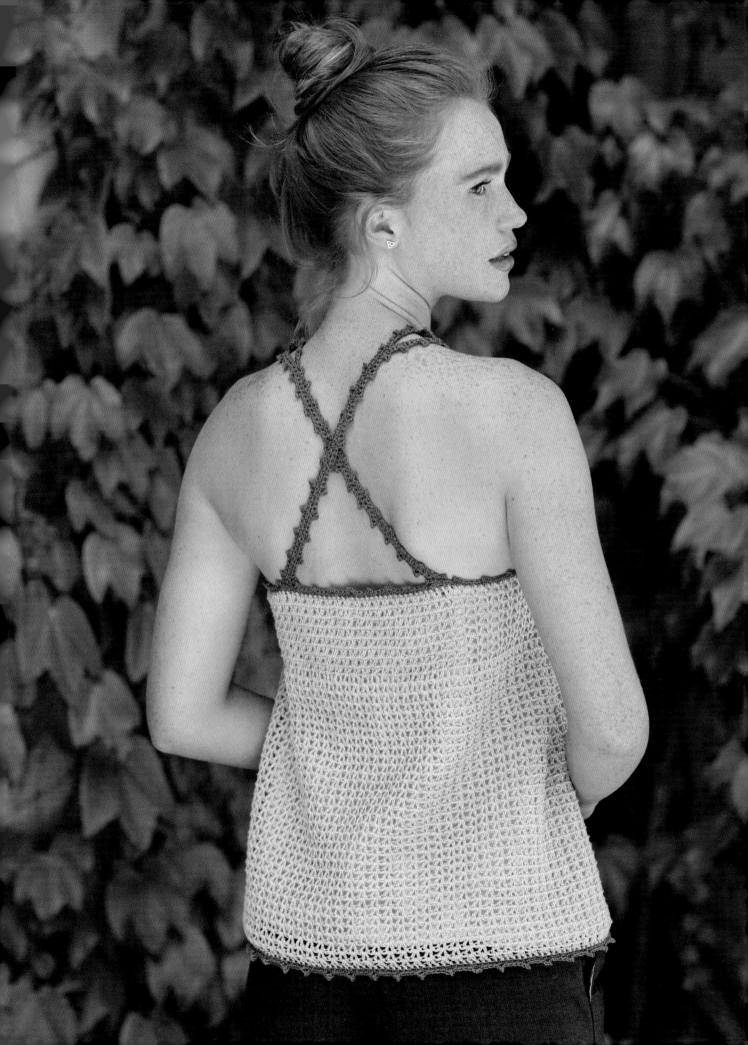

8-sc arch**, ch 2, sc in center sc of next 5-sc arch, ch 2; rep from * across, ending last rep at **, sc in each rem sc of last arch, turn.

Row 2: Ch 1, sc across, working sc in each sc, 3 sc in each ch-3 sp, 2 sc in each ch-2 sp, at end of row, work sc in last st, sc in next sc on body edging, turn.

Row 3: (RS) *Picot, sc in next 4 sc; rep from * across, at end of necklace piece, rotate piece, work 6 sc in row-ends down side of necklace edge, turn.

Row 4: Ch 1, sc in first 3 sc, (ch 3, sl st, ch 7, sl st, ch 3, sl st) in same sp, sc in rem 3 sc, ch 7, turn, qtr (see Stitch Guide) in first sc of current row, ch 51 for strap, turn.

Row 5: (WS) Sk first ch, sc in next 50 ch, 10 sc in ch-7 sp, sl st in edge of necklace piece, turn—60 sc for strap.

Row 6: (RS) Working down outside of strap, *picot, sc in next 4 sc; rep from * across, work 2 sc in row-end of strap to turn corner, rotate piece to work along foundation ch side of strap, **picot, sc in next 4 sc; rep from ** across inside of strap

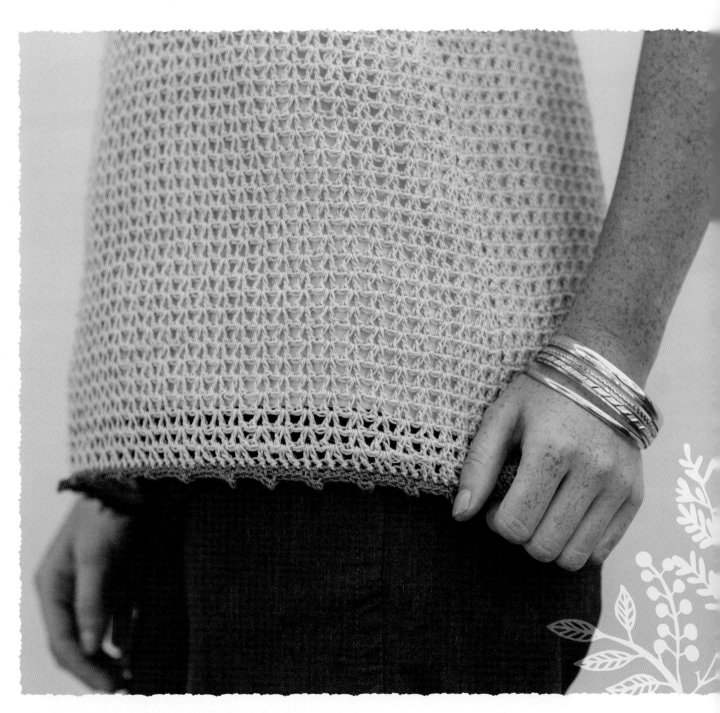

and over qtr for same number of picots as outside edge, at end of row, join with sl st to necklace piece. Fasten off.

With WS facing, rep instructions for other side.

Cross straps in back and pin equidistant from center back about 7" (18 cm) apart or as desired. Using tapestry needle and CC, sew straps to back edging.

HEM EDGING

With RS facing and larger hook, join CC at side seam of hem.

Rnd 1: (RS) Ch 1, sc in each dc around, sl st in first sc to join—180 (196, 212, 228, 244) sc. Do not turn.

Rnd 2: Ch 1, sc in same sp, sc in next 3 sc, *picot, sc in next 4 sc; rep from * around, sl st in first sc to join. Fasten off.

Weave in ends.

LINING (OPTIONAL)

If using lining, trace bodice of garment onto lining with ¾" (2 cm) of seam allowance. Cut out lining, form a tube, and sew sides together. Fold edges to inside of tube twice to hide raw edges inside fold and sew around all edges. Sew lining into garment with seams on the inside to not show through top.

Steam block gently.

Reduced Necklace & Body Edging Join

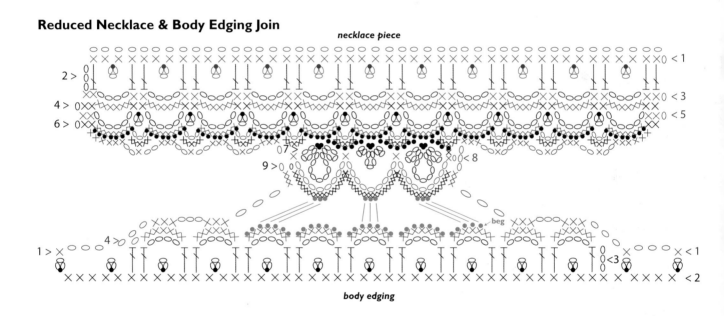

necklace piece

body edging

Stitch Key

● = slip stitch (sl st)

○ = chain (ch)

✕ = single crochet (sc)

🇮 = double crochet (dc)

🎔 = picot

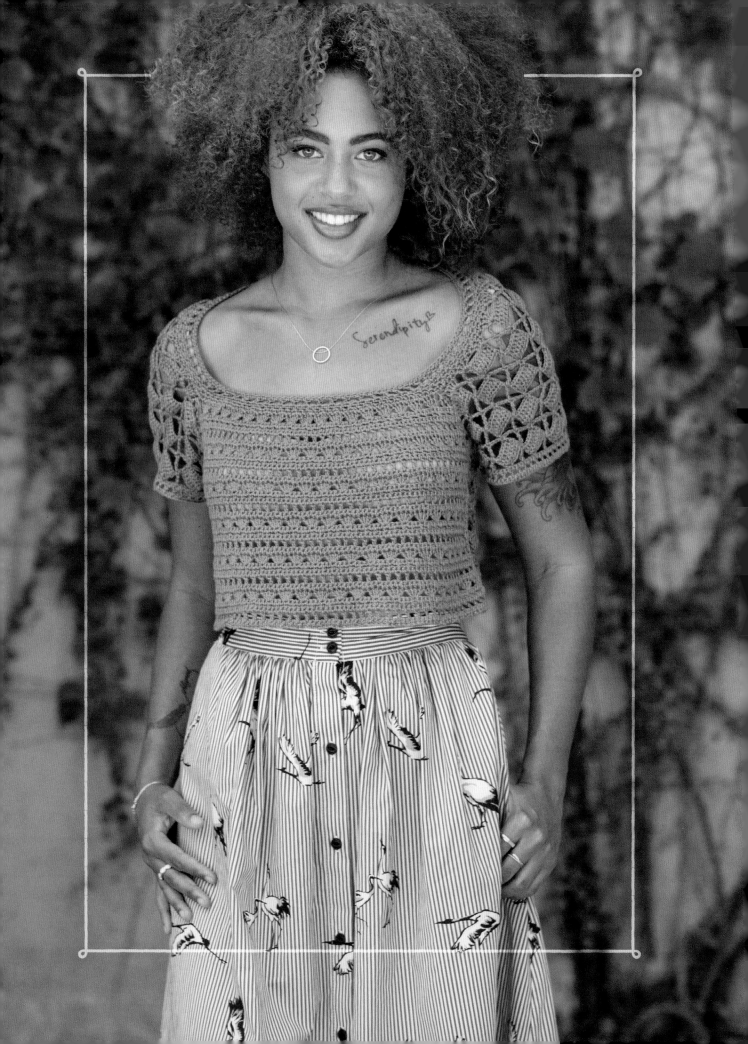

kinzie tee

This cropped tee showcases beautiful linen yarn in a cool geometric pattern. It features raglan-sleeve construction with a keyhole detail in the back and is a great weight for warmer weather.

FINISHED SIZE

About 37 (41½, 45½, 48½, 51½)" (94 [105.5,115.5, 123, 131] cm) bust circumference.

Tee shown measures 37" (94 cm).

YARN

Sportweight (#2 Fine).

Shown here: Louet North America Euroflax (100% wet-spun linen; 270 yd [246 m]/3½ oz [100 g]): #1823741 shamrock, 2 (3, 3, 4, 4) skeins.

HOOK

Size C/2 (2.75 mm) and G/6 (4 mm).

Adjust hook size if necessary to obtain correct gauge.

NOTIONS

Tapestry needle; markers (m).

GAUGE

22 sts and 18 rows = 4" (10 cm) in main body patt with larger hook, blocked.

3 diamonds and 6 rows = 4" (10 cm) with smaller hook, blocked.

STITCH GUIDE

FAN
4 dc in indicated st or sp.

RIGHT FRONT NECK CORNER
Yo, insert hook in next st, yo, pull up lp, yo and draw through 2 lps on hook (2 lps on hook), sk next 2 sc, yo twice, insert hook in next sc, yo, pull up lp, [yo and draw through 2 lps on hook] twice (3 lps on hook), yo twice, insert hook in 2nd dc from top corner of first diamond on sleeve, yo, pull up lp, [yo and draw through 2 lps on hook] twice (4 lps on hook), sk next dc, yo, insert hook in top of corner of diamond, yo, pull up lp, yo and draw through 2 lps on hook (5 lps on hook), yo and draw through all lps on hook—1 lp rem.

LEFT FRONT NECK CORNER
Yo, insert hook in next st, yo, pull up lp, yo and draw through 2 lps on hook (2 lps on hook), sk next dc, yo twice, insert hook in next dc of last diamond, yo, pull up lp, [yo and draw through 2 lps on hook] twice (3 lps on hook), yo twice, insert hook in first sc of front, yo, pull up lp, [yo and draw through 2 lps on hook] twice (4 lps on hook), sk next dc, yo, insert hook in next sc, yo, pull up lp, yo and draw through 2 lps on hook (5 lps on hook), yo and draw through all lps on hook—1 lp rem.

Back

With larger hook, ch 93 (105, 117, 125, 133).

Row 1: (WS) Working in back bump of ch, sc in 2nd ch from hook and in each ch across—92 (104, 116, 124, 132) sc, turn.

Row 2: (RS) Ch 3, sk first sc, *dc in next sc, ch 1, sk next sc; rep from * across, ending with dc in last sc, turn—45 (51, 57, 61, 65) ch-1 sps.

Row 3: Ch 1, sc in each dc and ch-1 sp across, ending with sc in top of tch, turn—92 (104, 116, 124, 132) sc.

Row 4: Ch 1, sc in first sc, [ch 1, sk next sc, sc in next sc] across to last sc, sc in last sc, turn—45 (51, 57, 61, 65) ch-1 sps.

Row 5: Ch 1, sc in each sc and ch-1 sp across, turn—92 (104, 116, 124, 132) sc.

Row 6: Ch 3, 2 dc in first sc, [sk next 3 sc, fan (see Stitch Guide) in next sc] across to last 3 sc, sk next 2 sc, 2 dc in last st, turn—22 (25, 28, 30, 32) fans.

Row 7: Ch 1, sc in each dc across, turn—92 (104, 116, 124, 132) sc.

Rows 8–25: Rep Rows 2–7 three times.

Row 26: Rep Row 2. Fasten off.

Front

Work as for back. Do not fasten off.

SHAPE ARMHOLES
Row 27: (WS) Sl st in first dc and ch-1 sp, sc in each dc and ch-1 sp across to last ch-1 sp, sc in last ch-1 sp, turn, leaving last 2 sts unworked—88 (100, 112, 120, 128) sc rem.

Row 28: Rep Row 4 of back but leave last st unworked, turn—1 st dec'd.

Row 29: Ch 1, sc in each sc and ch-1 sp across to last st, turn, leaving last st unworked—86 (98, 110, 118, 126) sc rem.

Row 30: Ch 3, 2 dc in first sc, [sk next 3 sc, fan in next sc] across to last 5 sc, sk next 3 sc, 2 dc in next st, turn, leaving last st unworked—20 (23, 26, 28, 30) fans rem.

Row 31: Sl st in first 2 dc, sc in each dc across to last 2 dc, turn, leaving last 2 dc unworked—82 (94, 106, 114, 122) sts rem.

Row 32: Rep Row 2 of back.

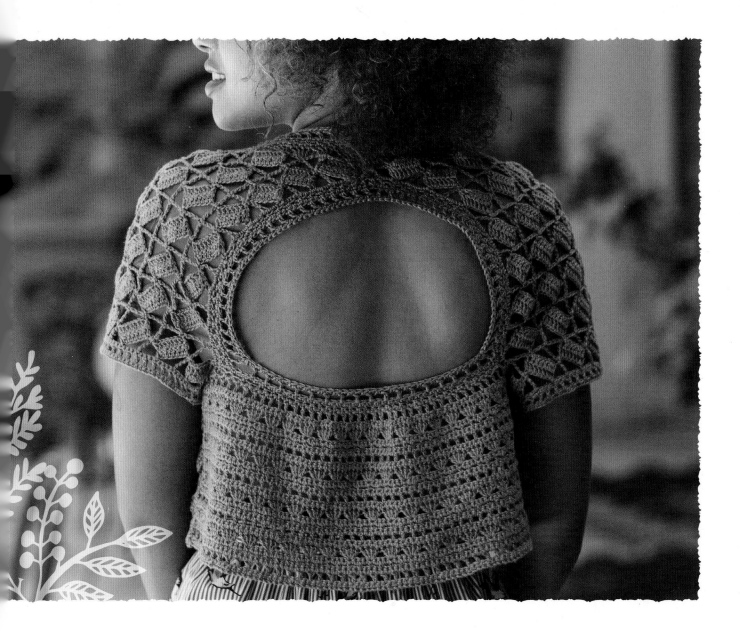

Rows 33–35: Rep Rows 27–29—76 (88, 100, 108, 116) sc rem. Fasten off.

Sleeve (Make 2)

With smaller hook, ch 81 (89, 97, 105, 113).

Row 1: (WS) Working in back bump of ch, sc in 2nd ch from hook and in each ch across—80 (88, 96, 104, 112) sc, turn.

Row 2: (RS) Ch 3, sk first sc, [dc in next sc, ch 1, sk next sc] across to last sc, dc in last sc, turn.

Row 3: Ch 1, sc in each dc and ch-1 sp across, ending with sc in top of tch, turn.

Row 4: Ch 10, sk first 4 sc, *sl st in next sc, ch 3, turn, dc in next 7 ch, turn, ch 3, sk first dc, dc in next 6 dc, dc in top of tch**, sk next 3 sc, dtr in next sc, ch 7, sk next

3 sc; rep from * across, ending last rep at **, dtr in last sc, turn—10 (11, 12, 13, 14) diamonds made.

Row 5: Ch 6, [sk next 7 dc, sc in top of tch (corner of diamond), ch 3, dtr in next dtr, ch 3] across, ending with dtr in 3rd ch of beg ch-10, turn.

SHAPE ARMHOLE

Row 6 (dec): Ch 1, 3 sc in first ch-3 sp, sc in next sc, 3 sc in next ch-3 sp, sc in next dtr, ch 10, *sk next ch-3 sp, sl st in next sc, ch 3, turn, dc in next 7 ch, turn, ch 3, sk first dc, dc in next 6 dc, dc in top of tch, sk next ch-3 sp, dtr in next dtr, ch 7; rep from * across to last dtr, dtr in last dtr, turn, leaving last diamond unworked—8 (9, 10, 11, 12) diamonds rem.

Row 7: Sl st in next 7 dc and in top of tch, ch 3, *dtr in next dtr, ch 3, sc in top corner of diamond, ch 3; rep from * across, dtr in 3rd ch of beg ch-10, turn.

Row 8 (dec): Ch 10, *sk next ch-3 sp, sl st in next sc, ch 3, turn, dc in next 7 ch, turn, ch 3, sk first dc, dc in next 6 dc, dc in top of tch, sk next ch-3 sp, dtr in next dtr, ch 7; rep from * across to last dtr, dtr in last dtr, turn, leaving last diamond unworked—1 diamond dec'd.

Rows 9–14 (16, 18, 20, 22): Rep Rows 7 and 8 three (four, five, six, seven) times—4 diamonds rem.

Row 15 (17, 19, 21, 23): Rep Row 7.

Row 16 (18, 20, 22, 24): Ch 10, *sk next ch-3 sp, sl st in next sc, ch 3, turn, dc in next 7 ch, turn, ch 3, sk first dc, dc in next 6 dc, dc in top of tch, sk next ch-3 sp, dtr in next dtr**, ch 7, rep from * to **, ch 5, sk next ch-3 sp, sl st in next sc, turn, leaving last 2 diamonds unworked—2 diamonds rem.

Row 17 (19, 21, 23, 25): Sl st in each ch of ch-5 sp, sl st in dtr, ch 6, sk next 7 dc, *sc in next top corner of diamond, ch 3**, dtr in dtr, ch 3, rep from * to **, dtr in 3rd ch of beg ch-10, turn.

Row 18 (20, 22, 24, 26): Ch 10, sk next ch-3 sp, sl st in next sc, ch 3, turn, dc in next 7 ch, turn, ch 3, sk first dc, dc in next 6 dc, dc in top of tch, sk next ch-3 sp, dtr in next dtr, turn, leaving last diamond unworked—1 diamond rem.

Row 19 (21, 23, 25, 27): Ch 6, sk next 7 dc, sc in next top corner of diamond, ch 3, dtr in 3rd ch of beg ch-10. Fasten off.

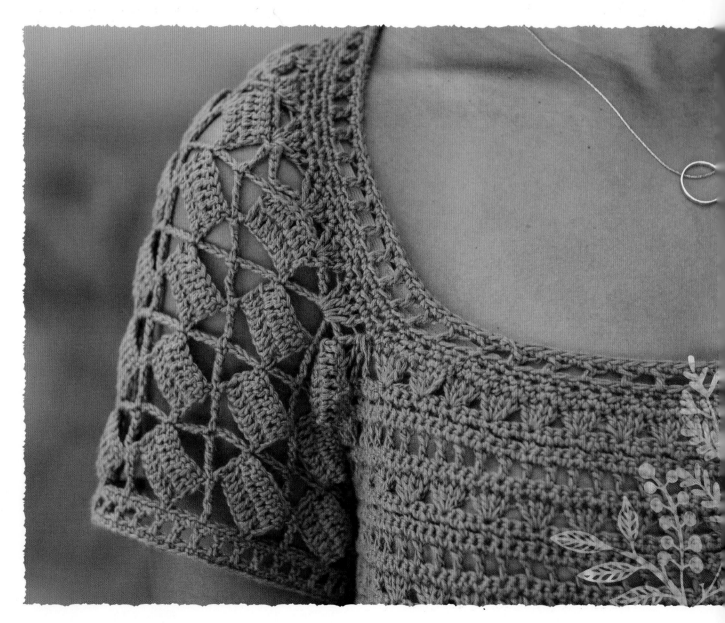

Diamonds

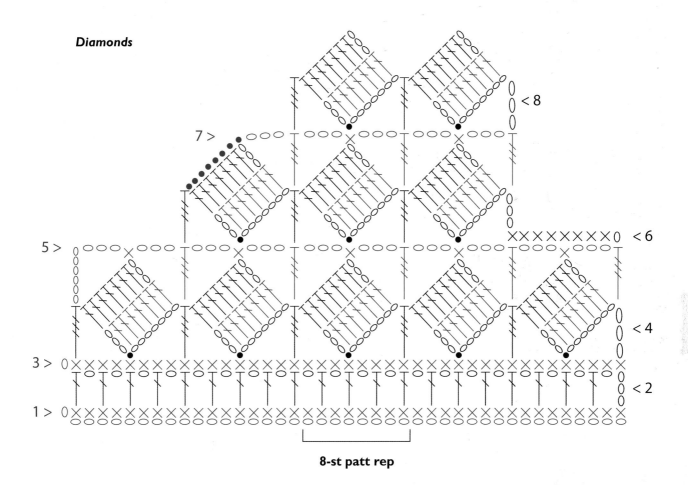

8-st patt rep

Stitch Key

● = slip stitch (sl st)

○ = chain (ch)

✕ = single crochet (sc)

⊤ = double crochet (dc)

⊤ = double treble (dtr)

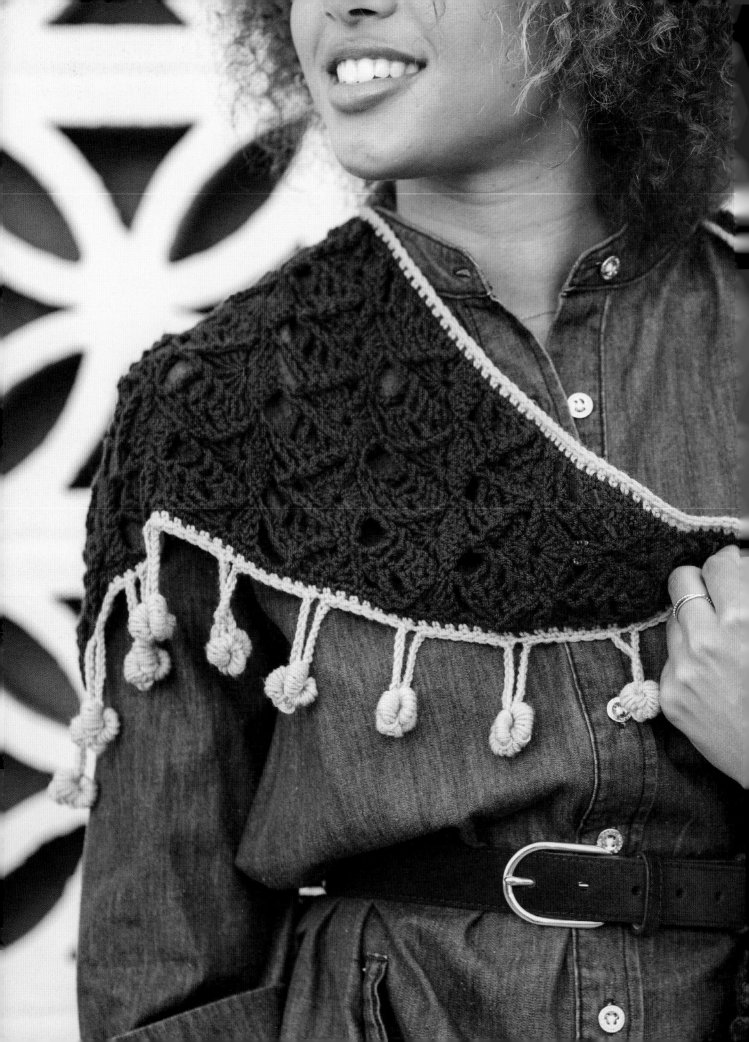

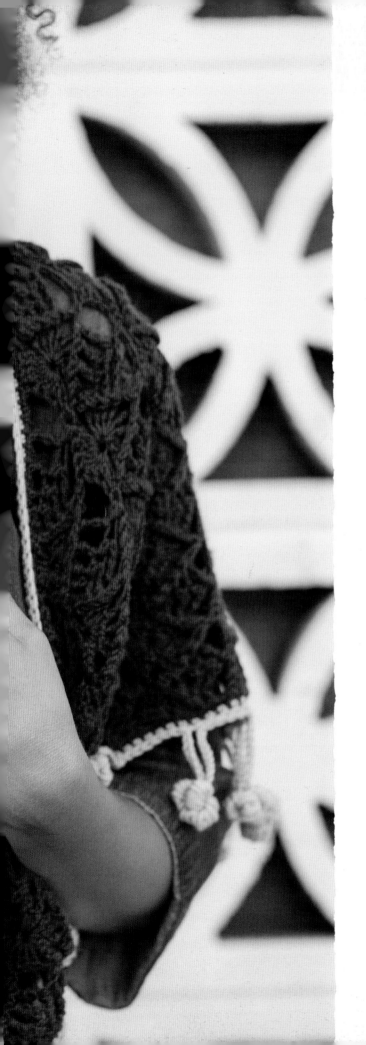

CHAPTER THREE

Mellow

Relax and flow with the changes of the seasons. As a chill creeps in making you crave warmth and layers, slip on some mitts, grab a richly textured bag, or wrap yourself in a captivating shawl. A layered look is the key to staying chic.

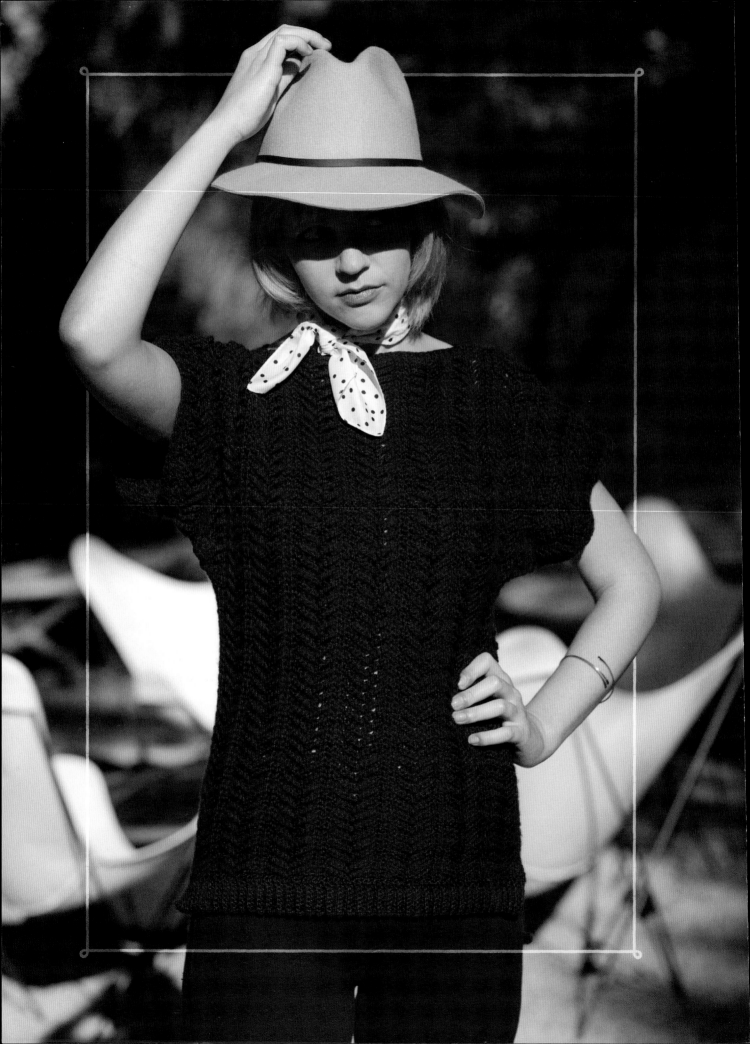

eastlake sweater

This is just the type of delicious texture I'm drawn to every fall. Eastlake is a dolman-sleeve sweater with a boat neck in a dimensional herringbone stitch. This sweater's simple silhouette and warmth make it the perfect layer for autumn.

FINISHED SIZE

32½ (37, 41½, 46, 55)" (82.5 [94, 105.5, 117, 139.5] cm) bust circumference.

Sweater shown measures 32½" (82.5 cm).

YARN

Worsted weight (#4 Medium).

Shown here: Berroco Vintage (52% acrylic, 40% wool, 8% nylon; 217 yd [198 m]/3½ oz [100 g]): #5182 black currant, 5 (5, 6, 6, 7) skeins.

HOOK

Size I/9 (5.5 mm).

Adjust hook size if necessary to obtain correct gauge.

NOTIONS

Tapestry needle.

GAUGE

2 herringbone columns (24 sts) and 11 herringbones (22 rows) = 4½" (11.5 cm).

NOTES

Sweater is worked in 2 pieces and seamed with a 3" (7.5 cm) side slit. Back is 3" (7.5 cm) longer than front.

Front

RIBBING

Ch 8.

Row 1: Working in back bump of ch, sc in 2nd ch from hook and in each ch across—7 sc, turn.

Row 2: Ch 1, sc blo in each sc across, turn.

Rows 3–87 (99, 111, 123, 147): Rep Row 2. Do not fasten off.

Rotate piece to work in row-ends of ribbing.

BODY

Row 1: (WS) Ch 1, sc in each row-end across—87 (99, 111, 123, 147) sc, turn.

Rows 2: Ch 1, sc in first sc, *ch 1, sk next sc, sc in next sc; rep from * across, turn.

Rows 3: Ch 1, sc in first sc, *ch 1, sc in next sc; rep from * across, turn.

Row 4: (RS) Ch 1, sc in first sc, ch 1, sc in next sc, *ch 5, sk next (ch-1 sp, sc, ch-1 sp, sc), working in front of last row, sc in next ch-1 sp 2 rows below, skipping ch-1 sp of current row, ch 5, sk next (sc, ch-1 sp, sc, ch-1 sp), sc in next sc, ch 1, sc in next sc; rep from * across, turn.

Row 5: Ch 1, sc in first sc, ch 1, sc in next sc, ch 1, *ignoring ch-5 sps of last row and working in skipped sts of 2 rows below, [dc in next sc 2 rows below, ch 1] 4 times, [sc in next sc on current row, ch 1] twice; rep from * across, ending with sc in last sc, turn—7 (8, 9, 10, 12) herringbone columns.

Row 6: Ch 1, sc in first sc, ch 1, sc in next sc, *ch 5, sk next (ch-1 sp, dc, ch-1 sp, dc), working in front of last row, sc in next ch-1 sp 2 rows below, skipping ch-1 sp of current row, ch 5, sk next (dc, ch-1 sp, dc, ch-1 sp), sc in next sc, ch 1, sc in next sc; rep from * across, turn.

Row 7: Ch 1, sc in first sc, ch 1, sc in next sc, ch 1, *ignoring ch-5 sps of last row and working in skipped sts of 2 rows below, [dc in next dc 2 rows below, ch 1] 4 times, [sc in next sc on current row, ch 1] twice; rep from * across, ending with sc in last sc, turn.

Rows 8–51: Rep Rows 6 and 7 twenty-two times.

SHAPE SLEEVES

Row 52: (RS) Rep Row 6, at end of row, ch 7, turn.

Row 53: Sc in 2nd ch from hook, [ch 1, sk next ch] 3 times, cont in patt as established (Row 7) across, at end of row, ch 7, turn—added half herringbone column to right sleeve.

Row 54: Sc in 2nd ch from hook, [ch 1, sk next ch, sc in next ch] 3 times, cont in patt (Row 6) across to last 3 ch-1 sps, ch 5, sl st in last ch-1 sp, sl st in last sc, turn—added half herringbone column to left sleeve.

Row 55: Ch 2, dc in first sc, ch 1, [dc in next sc, ch 1] twice, sc in next sc, cont as established across to last 3 ch-1 sps, [ch 1, dc in next sc] 3 times, turn.

Row 56: Sl st in first ch-1 sp 2 rows below, skipping ch-1 sp of current row, ch 5, sk next (dc, ch-1 sp, dc, ch-1 sp) of current row, sc in next sc, cont as established across to last 3 ch-1 sps, ch 5, sl st in first ch of tch, ch 7, turn.

Row 57: Sc in 2nd ch from hook, ch 1, sk next ch, sc in next ch, ch 1, sk next ch, dc in next ch, ch 1, sk next ch, dc in dc 2 rows below, cont as established to last 3 ch-1 sps, [ch 1, dc in next dc 2 rows below] 3 times, at end of row, ([ch 1, dc] 3 times) in same last dc, turn—2nd half of herringbone column added to right sleeve.

Row 58: Ch 1, sc in first dc, ch 1, sc in next dc, ch 5, sk next (ch-1 sp, dc, ch-1 sp, dc), working in front of last row, sc in next ch-1 sp 2 rows below, skipping ch-1 ch of current row, ch 5, sk next (dc, ch-1 sp, dc, ch-1 sp), sc in next sc, cont in patt across, at row end, ch 7, turn—2nd half of herringbone column added to left sleeve.

Rows 59–64: Rep Rows 53–58, but omit ch 7 at end of Row 58—11 (12, 13, 14, 16) herringbone columns; 2 columns each sleeve.

Rows 65–96: Rep [Row 7, then Row 6] sixteen times.

Row 97: Ch 1, sc in first sc, ch 1, sc in next sc, ch 1, *ignoring ch-5 sps of last row and working in skipped sts of 2 rows below, [sc in next dc 2 rows below, ch 1] 4 times, [sc in next sc on current row, ch 1] twice; rep from * across, ending with sc in last sc, turn.

Rows 98 and 99: Ch 1, sc in first sc, [ch 1, sc in next sc] across, turn. Fasten off.

Back

RIBBING

Work ribbing as for front.

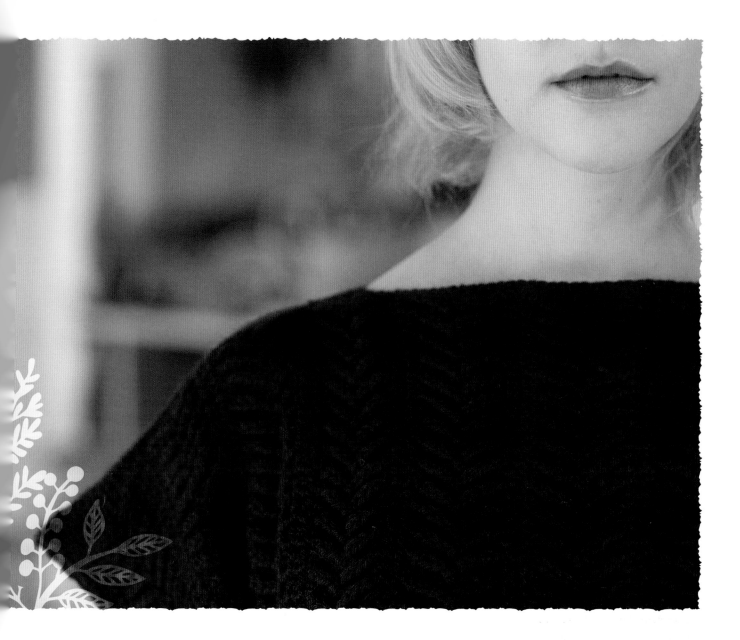

BODY

Work as for front to sleeve shaping, then rep Rows 6 and 7 seven more times. Cont with sleeve shaping and complete back as for front.

Finishing

With tapestry needle and using whipstitch, sew shoulder seams, leaving center 8½ (9, 10, 11, 12)" (21.5 [23, 25.5, 28, 30.5] cm) open for neck opening. Whipstitch sleeve and side seams, leaving the last 3" (7.5 cm) of front unsewn for side slits. Weave in ends. Steam block.

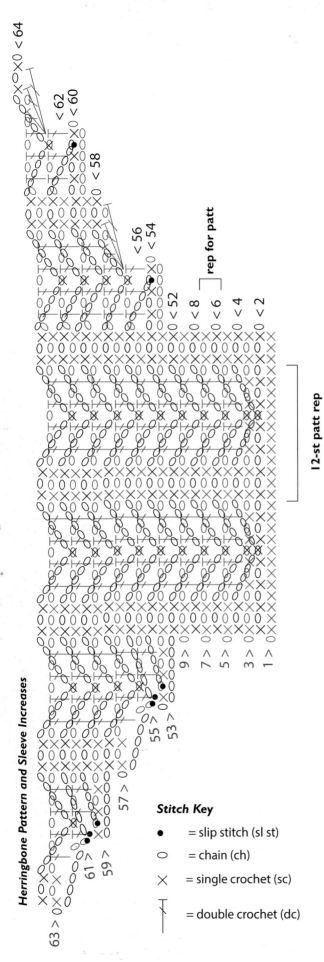

Herringbone Pattern and Sleeve Increases

64 > 62 > 60 < 58 < 56 < 54 < 52

rep for patt

< 8
< 6
< 4
< 2

12-st patt rep

9 >
7 >
5 >
3 >
1 >

55 >
53 >

57 >

63 > 61 > 59 >

Stitch Key

- ● = slip stitch (sl st)
- ○ = chain (ch)
- ✕ = single crochet (sc)
- ┬ = double crochet (dc)

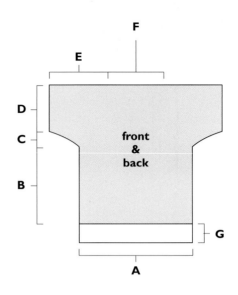

F

E

D

C

B

front & back

G

A

MEASUREMENTS

A: Front/back width
16¼ (18½, 20¾, 23, 27½)" (41.5 [47, 52.5, 58.5, 70] cm)

B: Front bottom edge to underarm
12" (30.5 cm)

C: Sleeve increase height
2¾" (7 cm)

D: Sleeve cuff height
7¼" (18.5 cm)

E: Shoulder/sleeve length
8¼ (9¼, 9¾, 10½, 12¼)" (21 [23.5, 25, 26.5, 31] cm)

F: Neck width
8½ (9, 10, 11, 12)" (21.5 [23, 25.5, 28, 30.5] cm)

G: Back extra length
3" (7.5 cm)

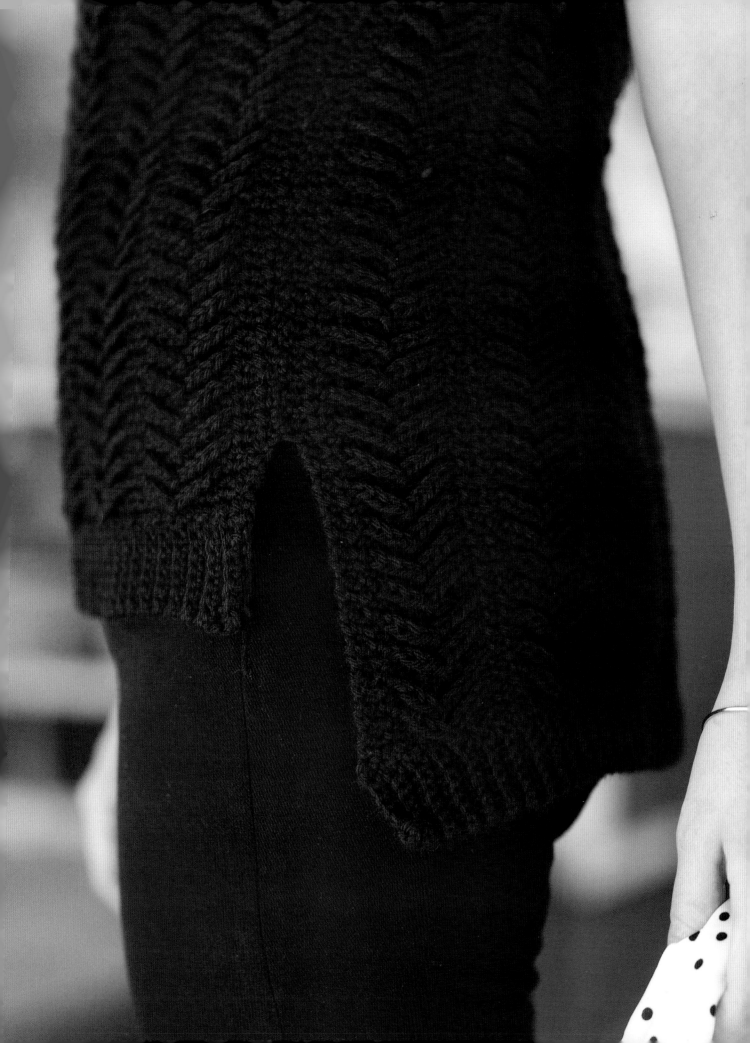

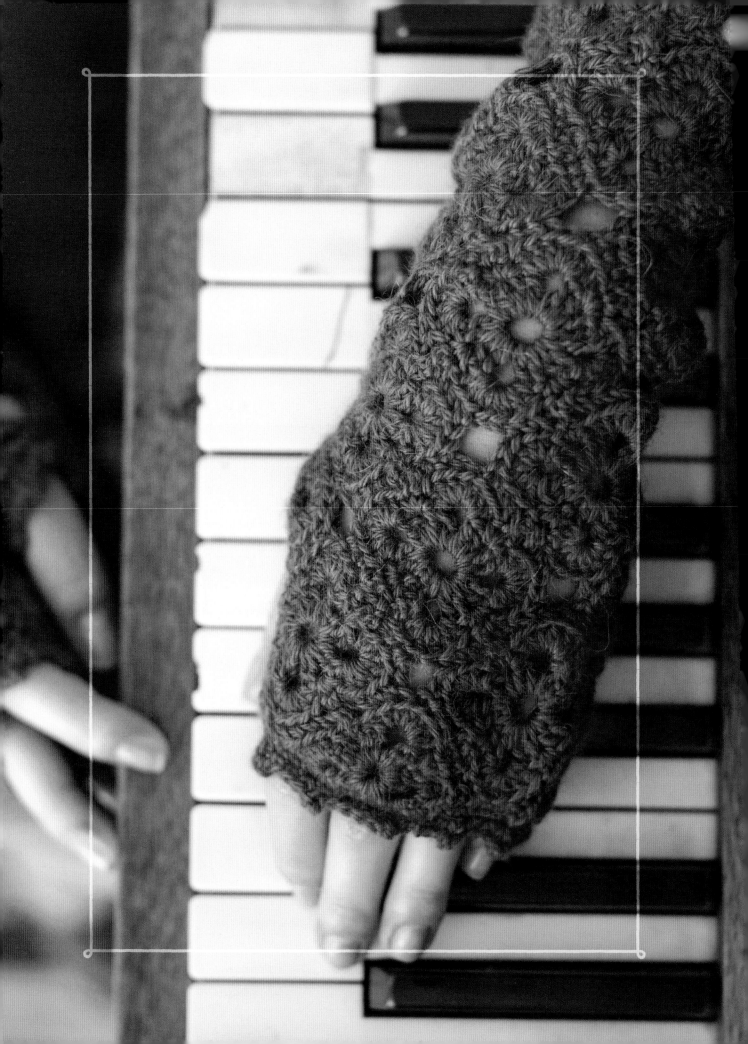

hazel mitts

These plush mitts are created by joining tiny motifs in a diamond pattern and finishing off with a pretty picot edging. They are worked in Blue Sky Fibers Royal, a truly luxurious yarn that yields the perfect fall accessory.

FINISHED SIZE

11" (28 cm) long (excluding picots) and 7" (18 cm) circumference.

YARN

Sportweight (#2 Fine).

Shown here: Blue Sky Fibers Royal (100% royal alpaca, 288 yd [263 m])]/3½ oz [100 g]): #711 vermilion, 1 skein.

HOOK

Size F/5 (3.75 mm).

Adjust hook size if necessary to obtain correct gauge.

NOTIONS

Tapestry needle.

GAUGE

One full motif = 2" (5 cm) square.

Mitt (Make 2)

FULL MOTIF (MAKE 20)

Ch 5, sl st in first ch to form a ring.

Rnd 1: (RS) Ch 3, (dc, ch 3, 2 dc) in ring, *ch 1, (2 dc, ch 3, 2 dc) in ring; rep from * twice, ch 1, sl st in top of beg ch-3. Do not turn.

Rnd 2: Sl st in next dc, sl st in next ch-3 sp, ch 3, 6 dc in same ch-3 sp, *(sc, ch 3, sc) in next ch-1 sp**, 7 dc in next ch-3 sp; rep from * around, ending last rep at **, sl st in top of beg ch-3. Fasten off.

HALF MOTIF (MAKE 8)

Ch 5, sl st in first ch to form a ring.

Row 1: (WS) Ch 5 (counts as dc, ch 2), 2 dc in ring, ch 1, (2 dc, ch 3, 2 dc) in ring, ch 1, (2 dc, ch 2, dc) in ring, turn.

Row 2: Sl st in first dc, sl st in next ch-2 sp, ch 3, 3 dc in same ch-2 sp, (sc, ch 3, sc) in next ch-1 sp, 7 dc in next ch-3 sp, (sc, ch 3, sc) in next ch-1 sp, 4 dc in last ch-2 sp. Fasten off.

ASSEMBLY

With RS facing, arrange motifs following assembly diagram. Using whipstitch, sew motifs together through the back lp only. Fold finished piece in half and sew the side seam, leaving the half motif open for thumb opening.

Finishing

TOP EDGING

With RS facing, join yarn anywhere around top of mitt.

Rnd 1: (RS) Ch 1, work 30 sc evenly around top of mitt, sl st in first sc to join. Do not turn.

Rnd 2: Ch 1, sc in same st, sc in each sc around, sl st in first sc to join.

Rnd 3: Ch 1, *sc in next 3 sc, picot; rep from * around, sl st in first sc to join—10 picots. Fasten off.

BOTTOM EDGING

With RS facing, join yarn anywhere around bottom of mitt.

Rnd 1: (RS) Ch 1, work 42 sc evenly around bottom of mitt, sl st in first sc to join. Do not turn.

Complete as for top edging, beg with Rnd 2.

THUMBHOLE EDGING

With RS facing, join yarn anywhere around thumbhole.

Rnd 1: (RS) Ch 1, work 18 sc evenly around thumbhole, sl st in first sc to join. Do not turn.

Complete as for top edging, beg with Rnd 2.

Weave in ends. Steam block gently.

Assembly

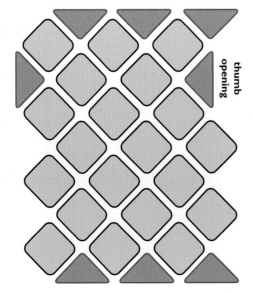

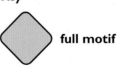

thumb opening

Key

full motif

half motif

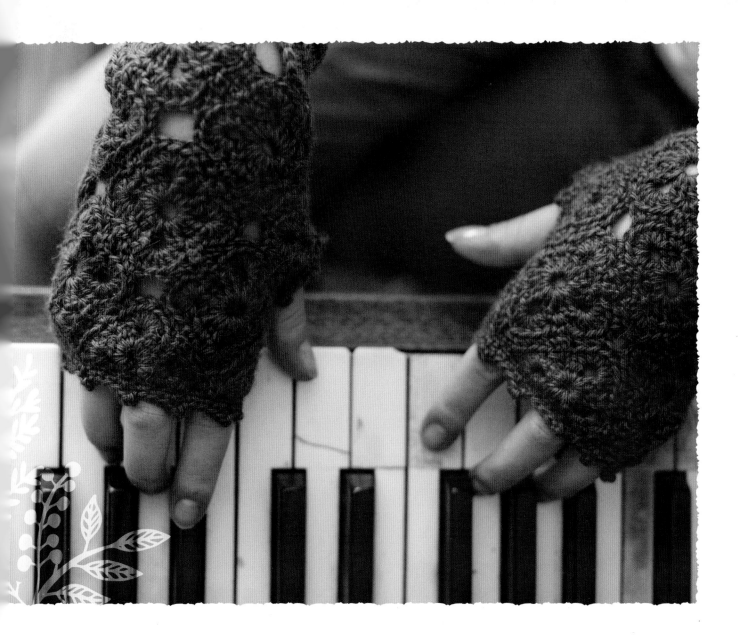

Full Motif

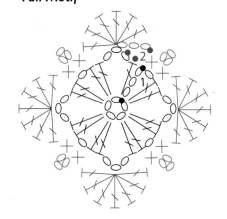

Half Motif

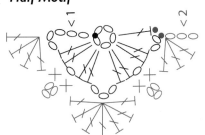

Stitch Key

● = slip stitch (sl st)

○ = chain (ch)

⊤ = double crochet (dc)

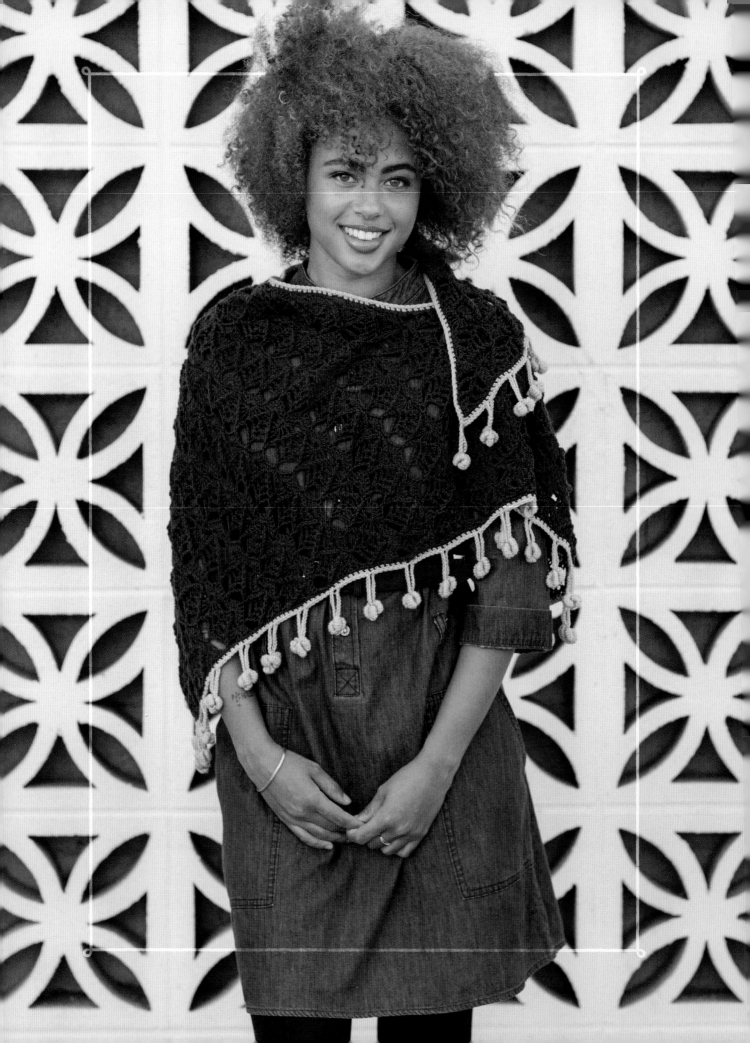

mayfield shawlette

I find the stitch pattern in this design absolutely captivating! It produces such a beautiful texture. This stitch is intriguing also because it has an odd number of rows yet a distinct right and wrong side; it switches between front and back post stitches to achieve this. The contrasting border tassels are a fun finishing detail. The two-stage blocking process may seem a little tedious, but the payoff is worth it. This isn't a pattern for beginners, but if you're up for the challenge, you'll be rewarded!

FINISHED SIZE
About 45" (114.5 cm) wide and 22" (56 cm) deep, excluding tassels.

YARN
DK weight (#3 Light).

Shown here: Lion Brand Superwash Merino (100% superwash merino; 306 yd [280 m]/3½ oz [100 g]): #145 eggplant (MC), 2 skeins; #123 hemp (CC), 1 skein.

HOOK
Size H/8 (5 mm) and F/5 (3.75 mm).

Adjust hook size if necessary to obtain correct gauge.

NOTIONS
Tapestry needle; pins for blocking.

GAUGE
3 pine tree stitches = 5" (12.5 cm) wide and 6 rows (2 pine tree rep) = 4" (10 cm) tall. First 7 rows of pattern make a triangle about 7" (18 cm) wide from side to side and 4½" (11.5 cm) tall at tallest point, blocked.

NOTE
To make the pine tree stitches, you will be working under the horizontal bars of the long stitches that are created from the yarn overs. This can be a little tricky to figure out at the beginning, but just remember that you are working in the previous stitch itself.

STITCH GUIDE

PINE TREE STITCH (PTS)

Ttr in indicated st or sp, ch 1, dtr in 4th horizontal bar of ttr just made, ch 1, tr in 3rd horizontal bar of dtr just made, ch 1, dc in 2nd horizontal bar of tr just made, ch 2, hdc in horizontal bar of dc just made, ch 1, dc in same 2nd horizontal bar of previous tr, ch 1, tr in same 3rd horizontal bar of previous dtr, ch 1, dtr in same 4th horizontal bar of previous ttr.

BACK POST TREBLE FOUR TOGETHER (BPTR4TOG)

*Yo twice, insert hook around post of next st from back to front to back, pull up a lp, [yo, pull through 2 lps on hook] twice; rep from * 3 times, yo, draw through all lps on hook—1 lp rem on hook.

BACK POST TREBLE EIGHT TOGETHER (BPTR8TOG)

Work as for BPtr4tog but rep from * 7 times instead of 3 times.

FRONT POST TREBLE FOUR TOGETHER (FPTR4TOG)

*Yo twice, insert hook around post of next st from front to back to front, pull up a lp, [yo, pull through 2 lps] twice, rep from * 3 more times, yo, draw through all lps on hook—1 lp rem on hook.

FRONT POST TREBLE EIGHT TOGETHER (FPTR8TOG)

Work as for FPtr4tog but rep from * 7 times instead of 3 times.

PUFF BOBBLE (PB)

Yo, [draw up lp from under indicated ch, yo] 9 times, yo, pull through all lps on hook.

TASSEL

Ch 13, work PB (see above) over last 3 ch, ch 4, work PB over just made ch-4, sl st in 10th ch from beg of ch-13, ch 3, work PB over just made ch-3, sl st bet first and 2nd PB, ch 3, PB over just made ch-3, sl st in 10th ch again, ch 10.

Shawl

With MC and larger hook, ch 5, sl st in first ch to form a ring.

Row 1: (WS) Ch 3 (counts as dc throughout), 6 dc in ring, turn—7 dc.

Row 2: (Ch 3, 3 dc) in first dc, sc in next dc, sk next dc, 7 dc in next dc, sk next dc, sc in next dc, 4 dc in last dc, turn.

Row 3 (pine trees): Ch 1, sc in first dc, ch 1, pts (see Stitch Guide) in next sc, ch 1, sk next 3 dc, sc in next dc (center st of 7-dc group), ch 1, pts in next sc, ch 1, sk next 3 dc, sc in last dc, turn—2 pine trees.

Row 4: Ch 4, BPtr4tog (see Stitch Guide) around first 4 arms of pts, ch 4, sc in next ch-2 sp at top of pts, ch 4, BPtr8tog (see Stitch Guide) around rem 4 arms of current pts and around first 4 arms of next pts, ch 4, sc in next ch-2 sp at top of current pts, ch 4, BPtr4tog around rem 4 arms of pts, turn.

Row 5: Ch 3, 3 dc in first BPtr4tog, sc in first ch of next ch-4 sp, 7 dc in next sc, sc in next BPtr8tog, 7 dc in next sc, sc in last ch of next ch-4 sp, 4 dc in last st, turn.

Row 6 (pine trees): Ch 1, sc in first dc, *ch 1, pts in next sc, ch 1, sk next 3 dc, sc in next dc; rep from * across, turn—3 pine trees.

Row 7: Ch 4, FPtr4tog (see Stitch Guide) around first 4 arms of first pts, ch 4, sc in next ch-2 sp at top of pts, ch 4, *FPtr8tog (see Stitch Guide) around rem 4 arms of current pts and around first 4 arms of next pts, ch 4, sc in next ch-2 sp, ch 4; rep from * across, FPtr4tog around rem 4 arms of last pts, turn.

Row 8: Ch 3, 3 dc in first FPtr4tog, sk next ch-4 sp, sc in next sc, 7 dc in next FPtr8tog, sc in 2nd ch of next ch-4 sp, 7 dc in next sc, sc in next FPtr8tog, 7 dc in next ch-4 sp, sc in next sc, 4 dc in last FPtr4tog, turn.

Row 9 (pine trees): Rep Row 6—4 pine trees.

Row 10: Ch 4, BPtr4tog around first 4 arms of first pts, ch 4, sc in next ch-2 sp at top of pts, ch 4, *BPtr8tog around rem 4 arms of current pts and around first 4 arms of next pts, ch 4, sc in next ch-2 sp, ch 4; rep from * across, BPtr4tog around rem 4 arms of last pts, turn.

Row 11: Ch 3, 3 dc in first BPtr4tog, sk next ch-4 sp, sc in next sc, *7 dc in next BPtr8tog, sc in 2nd ch of next ch-4 sp, 7 dc in next sc, sc in next FPtr8tog, 7 dc in next ch-4 sp, sc in next sc; rep from * across, 4 dc in last FPtr4tog, turn.

Row 12 (pine trees): Rep Row 6—6 pine trees.

Row 13: Rep Row 7.

Row 14: Ch 3, 3 dc in first st, *sc in 2nd ch of next ch-4, 7 dc in next sc, sc in next FPtr8tog, 7 dc in next ch-4 sp, sc in next sc, 7 dc in next FPtr8tog; rep from * across, 4 dc in FPtr4tog, turn.

Rows 15–17: Rep Rows 9–11—9 pine trees.

Row 18 (pine trees): Rep Row 6—12 pine trees.

Row 19: Rep Row 7.

Row 20: Ch 3, 3 dc in first st, *sk next ch-4, sc in next sc, 7 dc in next FPtr8tog; rep from * across, 4 dc in last FPtr4tog, turn.

Rows 21–23: Rep Rows 9–11—12 pine trees.

Rows 24–26: Rep Rows 18–20—18 pine trees.

Rows 27 and 28: Rep Rows 9 and 10—18 pine trees.

Row 29: Ch 3, 3 dc in first st, *sk next ch-4, sc in next sc, 7 dc in next BPtr8tog; rep from * across, 4 dc in last BPtr4tog, turn.

Rows 30–32: Rep Rows 18–20—18 pine trees.

FIRST SHAWL TIP

Row 1 (short row): (WS) Rep Row 6 of shawl, working only 6 rep, turn—6 pine trees.

Row 2: Ch 1, sc bet 2nd and 3rd arm of first pts, ch 3, sc in next ch-2 sp at top of pts, ch 4, *BPtr8tog around 4 arms of current pts and around first 4 arms of next pts, ch 4, sc in next ch-2 sp, ch 4; rep from * across, BPtr4tog around rem 4 arms of last pts, turn.

Row 3: Rep Row 20 of shawl, ending with sc in sc at top of last pine tree, turn.

Row 4: Rep Row 6 of shawl—5 pine trees.

Row 5: Rep Row 7, ending with FPtr8tog, ch 4, sc in last ch-2 sp, turn, leaving rem 4 arms of last pts unworked.

Row 6: Ch 1, *7 dc in next FPtr8tog, sc in next sc; rep from * across, 4 dc last FPtr4tog, turn.

Row 7: Rep Row 6 of shawl, working only 4 rep, turn—4 pine trees.

Rows 8–12: Rep Rows 2–6—3 pine trees.

Row 13: Rep Row 6 of shawl, working only 2 rep, turn—2 pine trees.

Row 14: Ch 1, sc bet 2nd and 3rd arm of first pts, ch 3, sc in next ch-2 sp at top of pts, ch 4, BPtr8tog around rem 4 arms of current pts and around first 4 arms of next pts, ch 4, sc in next ch-2 sp, turn.

Row 15: Ch 3, 3 dc in first st, sc in next BPtr8tog, 4 dc in last st, turn.

Row 16: Ch 1, sc in first dc, ch 1, pts in next sc, sc in top of beg ch-3—1 pine tree. Fasten off.

SECOND SHAWL TIP

Row 1: With WS facing, sk next 5 unworked 7-dc groups from beg of first tip in center of the shawl, join yarn in 4th dc (center dc) of next 7-dc group, ch 1, sc in same st, then work only 6 reps of Row 6 of shawl across, turn—6 pine trees.

Row 2: Rep Row 10 of shawl, ending with BPtr8tog, ch 4, sc in last ch-2 sp, turn, leaving rem 4 arms of last pts unworked.

Row 3: Ch 1, *7 dc in next BPbptr8tog, sc in next sc; rep from * across, 4 dc last BPtr4tog, turn.

Row 4: Rep Row 6 of shawl, working only 5 rep, turn—5 pine trees.

Row 5: Ch 1, sc bet 2nd and 3rd arm of first pts, ch 3, sc in next ch-2 sp at top of pts, ch 4, *FPtr8tog around 4 arms of current pts and around first 4 arms of next pts, ch 4, sc in next ch-2 sp, ch 4; rep from * across, FPtr4tog around rem 4 arms of last pts, turn.

Row 6: Rep Row 20 of shawl, ending with sc in sc at top of last pts, turn.

Row 7: Ch 3, sk first 3 dc, sc in next dc, cont in patt as established (Row 6 of shawl) across, ending with sc in top of beg, ch-3, turn—4 pine trees.

Rows 8 and 9: Rep Rows 2 and 3.

Row 10: Rep Row 6 of shawl, working only 3 rep, turn—3 pine trees.

Rows 11–13: Rep Rows 5–7—2 pine trees.

Row 14: Ch 4, BPtr4tog around first 4 arms of first pts, ch 4, sc in next ch-2 sp, ch 4, BPtr8tog around rem 4 arms of current pts and around first 4 arms of last pts, turn, leaving rem 4 arms unworked, turn.

Row 15: Ch 1, 7 dc in first BPtr8tog, sc in next sc, 4 dc in last BPtr4tog, turn.

Row 16: Ch 1, sc in first dc, ch 1, pts in next sc, sk next 3 dc, sc in next dc—1 pine tree. Fasten off.

Finishing

Wet-block shawl, pin to measurements, and let dry completely.

EDGING AND TASSELS

With RS facing and larger hook, join MC in upper right corner of shawl tip.

Rnd 1: (RS) Ch 1, 3 sc in corner, work 66 sc evenly along top edge of shawl tip to the 7-dc group where shawl tip started, work sc in center dc and next 2 dc of this first 7-dc group, ch 3, [5 sc in center 5 dc of next 7-dc group, ch 3] 5 times across center shawl section to beg of next shawl tip, work sc in the 2 dc before center dc of next 7-dc group, sc in center dc of same group, work 66 sc evenly along top edge of next shawl tip, 3 sc in corner, work about 125 sc evenly down outside edge to bottom tip, 3 sc in center point, work another 125 sc evenly up other outside edge to tip, sl st in first sc to join. Fasten off.

Rnd 2: With RS facing, join CC in center sc of top right corner, ch 1, 3 sc in same st, sc in each sc and ch, working 3 sc in each corner, sl st in first sc to join. Do not fasten off.

Rnd 3 (tassels): Ch 1, 3 sc in center sc, sc in each sc across to next shawl point, ending with sc in last sc before center sc of corner, *change to smaller hook, (sc, tassel [see Stitch Guide], sc) in next sc, change back to larger hook, sc in next 6 sc; rep from * down outside edge of shawl to bottom tip, placing a tassel in center point (it's okay if tassels on each side of center tassel are a little closer/farther apart than normal), then cont up outside edge of shawl to corner, placing a tassel in center sc of corner, sl st in next sc to join. Fasten off.

Weave in ends. Steam block edging, pin, and let dry. Do not block tassels.

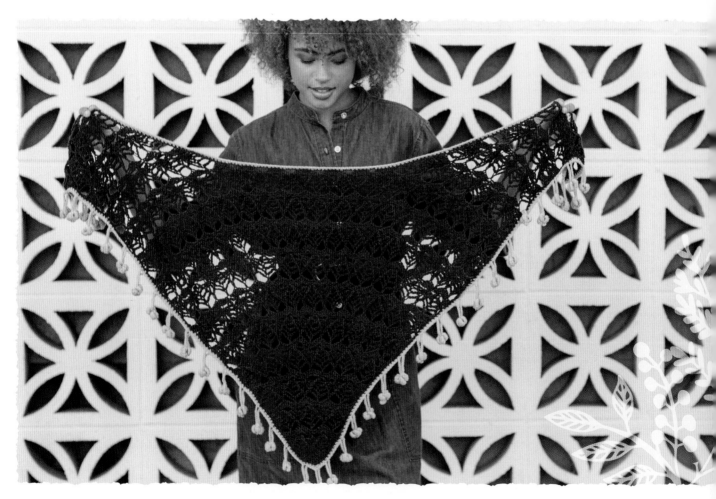

Beginning of Shawlette

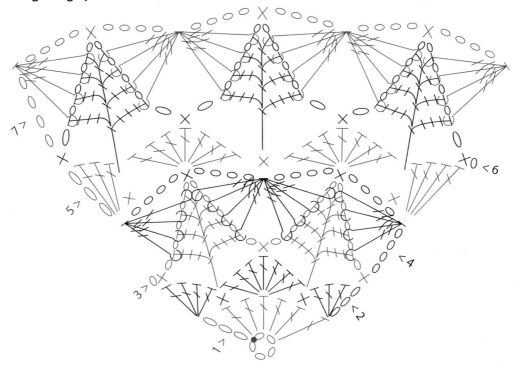

Stitch Key

- ● = slip stitch (sl st)
- ○ = chain (ch)
- ✕ = single crochet (sc)
- ⊤ = half double crochet (hdc)
- ⊤ = double crochet (dc)
- ⊤ = treble (tr)
- ⊤ = double treble (dtr)
- ⊤ = triple treble (ttr)

- ⊤ = front post treble (FPtr)
- ⊤ = back post treble (BPtr)

= pine tree stitch (pts)

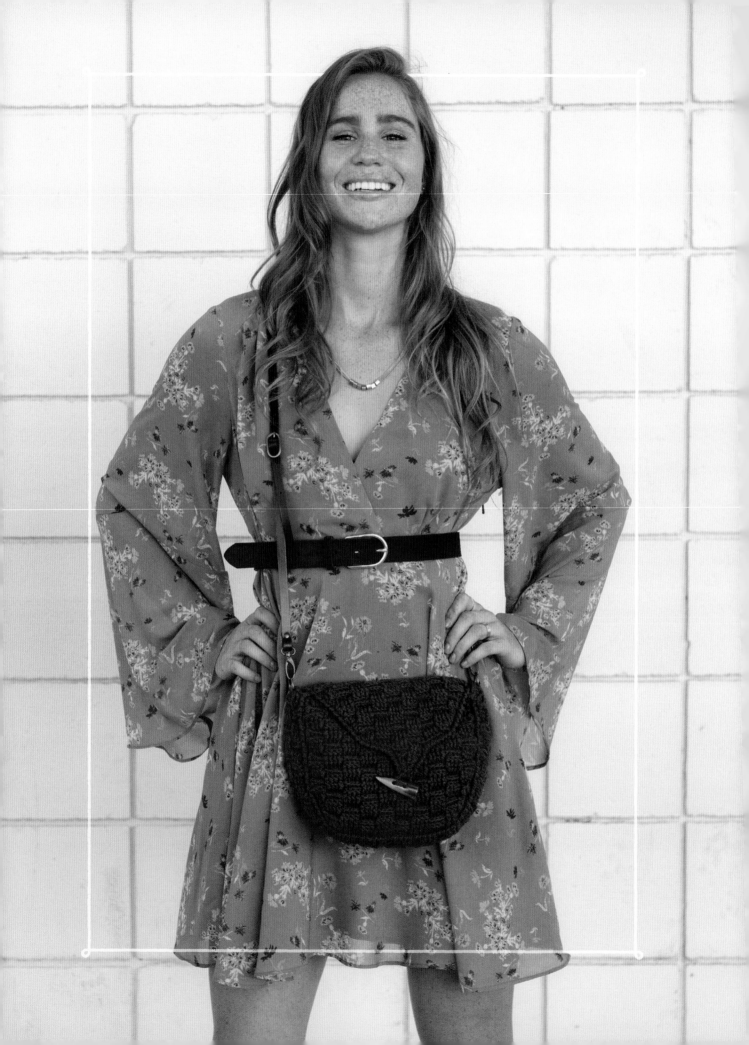

lockwood bag

This little bag is richly textured and perfectly understated. Worked in a basketweave stitch, the fabric is thick and sturdy, but the bag also has a sophisticated curve in the body and on the front flap. A tortoiseshell toggle is the perfect finish.

FINISHED SIZE

8" (20.5 cm) wide, 7" (18 cm) tall, and 2½" (6.5 cm) deep.

YARN

Worsted weight (#4 Medium).

Shown here: Spud & Chloe Sweater Worsted (55% wool, 45% organic cotton; 160 yd [145 m]/3½ oz [100 g]): #7511 chipmunk, 3 skeins.

HOOK

Size G/6 (4 mm).

Adjust hook size if necessary to obtain correct gauge.

NOTIONS

Tapestry needle; 2" (5 cm) toggle button; 40" (101.5 cm) bag handle; ½ yd (45.5 cm) lining fabric (optional); sewing needle and thread that matches yarn (if using lining).

GAUGE

20 sts and 14 rows = 4" (10 cm) in basketweave pattern.

NOTES

The turning chain (tch) at the beginning of each row does not count as a stitch. When working the edging, make sure to catch the turning chains and enclose them in the sc.

STITCH GUIDE

FRONT POST SINGLE CROCHET (FPSC)

Insert hook from front to back to front around post of corresponding stitch below, yo and pull up loop, yo and draw through 2 loops.

FRONT POST HALF DOUBLE CROCHET (FPHDC)

Yo, insert hook from front to back to front around post of corresponding stitch below, yo and pull up lp, yo and draw through all 3 lps on hook.

BACK POST HALF DOUBLE CROCHET (BPHDC)

Yo, insert hook from back to front to back around post of corresponding stitch below, yo and pull up lp, yo and draw through all 3 lps on hook.

BACK POST DOUBLE CROCHET (BPDC)

Yo, insert hook from back to front to back around post of stitch to be worked, yo and pull up lp [yo, draw through 2 lps on hook] twice.

FRONT POST DOUBLE CROCHET TWO TOGETHER (FPDC2TOG)

[Yo, insert hook from front to back to front around next st, pull up lp, yo, draw through 2 lps on hook] twice, yo, draw through all lps on hook—1 st dec'd.

FRONT POST DOUBLE CROCHET THREE TOGETHER (FPDC3TOG)

[Yo, insert hook from front to back to front around next st, pull up lp, yo, draw through 2 lps on hook] 3 times, yo, draw through all lps on hook—2 sts dec'd.

BACK POST DOUBLE CROCHET TWO TOGETHER (BPDC2TOG)

[Yo, insert hook from back to front to back around next st, pull up lp, yo, draw through 2 lps on hook] twice, yo, draw through all lps on hook—1 st dec'd.

BACK POST DOUBLE CROCHET/FRONT POST DOUBLE CROCHET TWO TOGETHER (BPDC/FPDC2TOG)

Yo, insert hook from back to front to back around next st, pull up lp, yo, draw through 2 lps on hook, yo, insert hook from front to back to front around next st, pull up lp, yo, draw through 2 lps on hook, yo, draw through all lps on hook—1 st dec'd.

Front

Ch 31.

Row 1: (WS) Dc in 4th ch from hook and in each ch across—28 dc, turn.

Row 2: Ch 3, 2 FPdc around first dc, FPdc around next dc, [BPdc around next 4 dc, FPdc around next 4 dc] 3 times, BPdc around next dc, 2 BPdc around last dc, turn—30 sts.

Row 3: Ch 3, 2 BPdc around first dc, BPdc around next 2 dc, [FPdc around next 4 dc, BPdc around next 4 dc] 3 times, FPdc around next 2 dc, 2 FPdc around last dc, turn—32 sts.

Row 4: Ch 3, FPdc around first dc, BPdc around same dc, BPdc around next 3 dc, [FPdc around next 4 dc, BPdc around next 4 dc] 3 times, FPdc around next 3 dc, FPdc around last dc, BPdc around same dc, turn—34 sts.

Row 5: Ch 3, 2 BPdc around first dc, [FPdc around next 4 dc, BPdc around next 4 dc] 4 times, 2 FPdc around last dc, turn—36 sts.

Row 6: Ch 3, 2 BPdc around first dc, BPdc around next dc, [FPdc around next 4 dc, BPdc around next 4 dc] 4 times, FPdc around next dc, 2 FPdc around last dc, turn—38 sts.

Row 7: Ch 3, 2 FPdc around first dc, FPdc around next 2 dc, [BPdc around next 4 dc, FPdc around next 4 dc] 4 times, BPdc around next 2 dc, 2 BPdc around last dc, turn—40 sts.

Row 8: Ch 3, [FPdc around next 4 dc, BPdc around next 4 dc] 5 times, turn.

Row 9: Ch 3, [BPdc around next 4 dc, FPdc around next 4 dc] 5 times, turn.

Row 10: Rep Row 9.

Rows 11 and 12: Rep Row 8.

Rows 13–22: Rep Rows 9–12 twice, then work Rows 9 and 10 once more. Do not fasten off.

EDGING

Next rnd: Rotate piece, ch 1, work 2 sc around post of last dc worked, then sc evenly in row-ends down the side, encasing tch (see Notes), sc in each foundation ch, sc evenly in row-ends up the other side, 3 sc in corner, sc in each dc across, sl st in first sc to join. Fasten off.

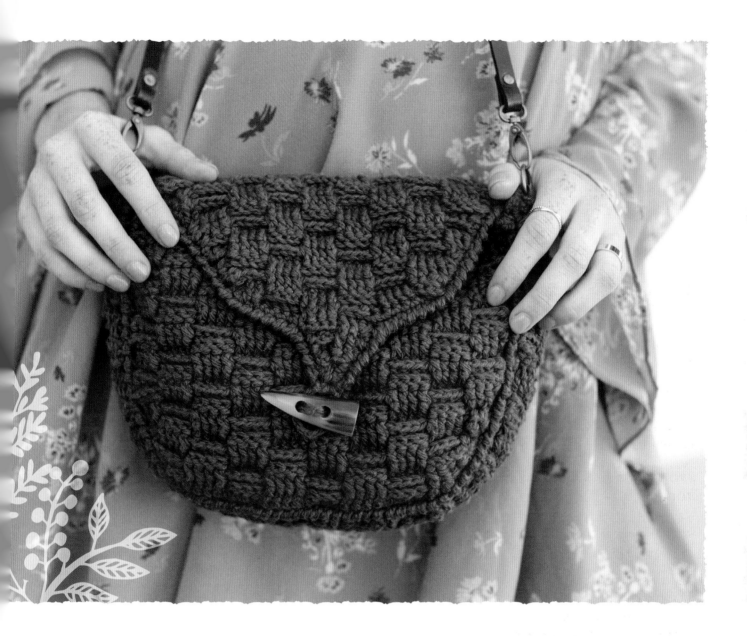

Back

Ch 31.

Rows 1–22: Work as for front.

Rows 23 and 24: Rep Row 8 of front.

Rows 25 and 26: Rep Row 9 of front. Do not fasten off.

FRONT FLAP

Row 1: (WS) Ch 3, sk first dc, FPdc around next 3 dc, [BPdc around next 4 dc, FPdc around next 4 dc] 4 times, BPdc around next 2 dc, BPdc2tog last 2 dc, turn—38 sts rem.

Row 2: Ch 3, sk first dc, FPdc around next 2 dc, [BPdc around next 4 dc, FPdc around next 4 dc] 4 times, BPdc around next dc, BPdc2tog last 2 dc, turn—36 sts rem.

Row 3: Ch 3, sk first dc, BPdc around next dc, [FPdc around next 4 dc, BPdc around next 4 dc] 4 times, FPdc2tog last 2 dc, turn—34 sts rem.

Row 4: Ch 3, sk first dc, [FPdc around next 4 dc, BPdc around next 4 dc] 4 times, turn, leaving last dc unworked—32 sts rem.

Row 5: Ch 3, sk first dc, BPdc around next 3 dc, [FPdc around next 4 dc, BPdc around next 4 dc] 3 times, FPdc around next 2 dc, FPdc2tog last 2 dc, turn—30 sts rem.

Row 6: Ch 3, sk first dc, BPdc around next 2 dc, [FPdc around next 4 dc, BPdc around next 4 dc] 3 times, FPdc around next dc, FPdc2tog last 2 dc, turn—28 sts rem.

Row 7: Ch 3, sk first dc, FPdc around next dc, [BPdc around next 4 dc, FPdc around next 4 dc] 3 times, BPdc2tog last 2 dc, turn—26 sts rem.

Row 8: Ch 3, sk first dc, [BPdc around next 4 dc, FPdc around next 4 dc] 3 times, turn, leaving last dc unworked—24 sts rem.

Row 9: Ch 3, sk first dc, FPdc around next 3 dc, [BPdc around next 4 dc, FPdc around next 4 dc] twice, BPdc around next 2 dc, BPdc2tog last 2 sts, turn—22 sts rem.

Row 10: Ch 3, sk first dc, FPdc around next 2 dc, [BPdc around next 4 dc, FPdc around next 4 dc] twice, BPdc around next dc, BPdc2tog last 2 sts, turn—20 sts rem.

Row 11: Sk first dc, BPsc around next dc, FPhdc around next dc, FPdc around next 3 dc, BPdc around next 4 dc, FPdc around next 4 dc, BPdc around next 3 dc, BPhdc around

next dc, FPsc around next dc, sl st in last dc—18 sts rem. Fasten off.

TAB

With RS facing, locate center 6 dc of front flap and join yarn in first st.

Row 1: (RS) Ch 3, FPdc around same dc and next 2 dc, BPdc around next 3 dc, turn, leaving rem sts unworked—6 sts.

Row 2: Ch 3, BPdc in first 3 dc, FPdc in last 3 dc, turn.

Row 3: Ch 3, BPdc2tog first 2 dc, BPdc/FPdc2tog next 2 dc, FPdc2tog last 2 dc, turn—3 sts rem.

Row 4: Ch 3, FPdc3tog—1 st rem. Do not fasten off.

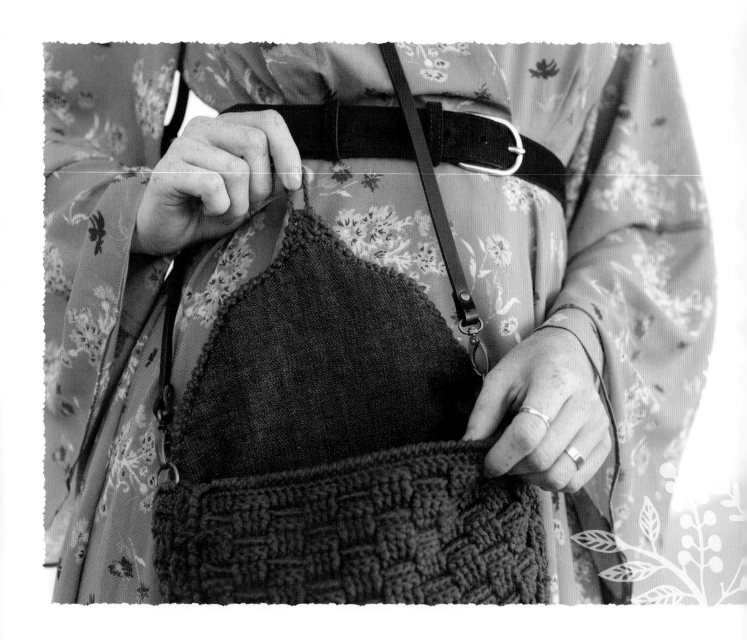

EDGING

Next rnd: Rotate piece, ch 1, sc evenly in row-ends down side of tab, sc in each dc across top edge of front flap, sc evenly in row-ends down side of flap and back, sc in each foundation ch across bottom edge, then sc evenly in row-end back up other side to top edge of front flap, sc in each dc across top edge, sc evenly in row-ends along side of tab, sl st in first sc to join. Fasten off.

Gusset

Ch 11.

Row 1: (RS) Dc in 4th ch from hook and in each ch across, turn—8 dc.

Row 2: Ch 3, BPdc around first 2 dc, FPdc around next 4 dc, BPdc around last 2 dc, turn.

Row 3 (inc): Ch 3, 2 FPdc around first dc, FPdc around next dc, BPdc around next 4 dc, FPdc around next dc, 2 FPdc around last dc, turn—10 dc.

Row 4: Ch 3, FPdc around first 3 dc, BPdc around next 4 dc, FPdc around last 3 dc, turn.

Row 5: Ch 3, BPdc around first 3 dc, FPdc around next 4 dc, BPdc around last 3 dc, turn.

Row 6: Rep Row 5.

Row 7 (inc): Ch 3, 2 FPdc around first dc, FPdc around next 2 dc, BPdc around next 4 dc, BPdc around next 2 dc, 2 BPdc around last dc, turn—12 dc.

Row 8: Ch 3, FPdc around first 4 dc, BPdc around next 4 dc, FPdc around last 4 dc, turn.

Row 9: Ch 3, BPdc around first 4 dc, FPdc around next 4 dc, BPdc around last 4 dc, turn.

Row 10: Rep Row 9.

Row 11: Rep Row 8.

Rows 12–54: Rep Rows 8–11 ten times, then work Rows 8–10 once more.

Row 55 (dec): Ch 3, sk first dc, FPdc around next 3 dc, BPdc around next 4 dc, FPdc around next 2 dc, BPdc2tog last 2 dc, turn—10 dc rem.

Rows 56–58: Rep Rows 4–6.

Row 59 (dec): Ch 3, sk first dc, FPdc around next 2 dc, BPdc around next 4 dc, FPdc around next dc, FPdc2tog last 2 dc, turn—8 dc rem.

Row 60: Ch 3, FPdc around first 2 dc, BPdc around next 4 dc, FPdc around last 2 dc, turn.

Row 61: Rep Row 2. Do not fasten off.

EDGING

Next rnd: Rotate piece, ch 1, work 2 sc around post of last dc worked, then sc evenly in row-ends down edge of piece, 3 sc in corner, sc in each foundation ch across bottom edge, 3 sc in corner, sc evenly in row-ends up other edge, 3 sc in corner, then sc in each dc across top edge, sl st in first sc to join. Fasten off.

Assembly

Wet-block all pieces and let them dry completely. Then, if using lining, trace pieces onto lining, cut out and assemble with a ¼" (6 mm) seam allowance (tracing around outside of piece will automatically add a seam allowance). Hold front of bag and gusset with WS together and pin in place. With RS facing, join yarn in top left corner of front, rsc across top edge of front, then for remaining edge around, work rsc through both thicknesses to join front and gusset together, sl st in first sc to join. Fasten off.

Add back to gusset and pin in place with WS held together. With RS facing, join yarn in right corner at beginning of gusset, work rsc through both thicknesses around sides and bottom to the end of the gusset, then rsc along front flap to the center point of tab, ch 10 (or more or fewer ch for your toggle button to fit through) for button loop, then continue rsc down other side to top of gusset, sl st in first rsc to join. Fasten off.

Weave in ends. For lining, hold right sides together and sew seams. Insert lining into bag, wrong sides together. Fold lining edges to WS and sew around top and flap with needle and thread to secure. Attach button to front of bag. Sew strap to top of gusset sides.

Gusset

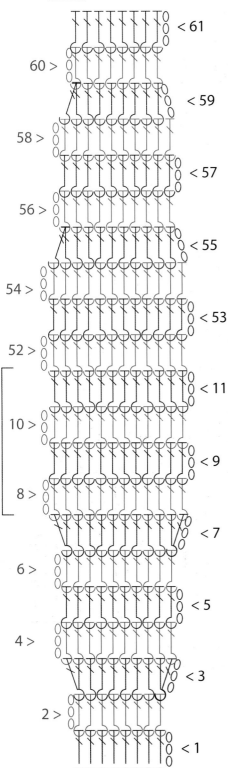

< 61
60 >
< 59
58 >
< 57
56 >
< 55
54 >
< 53
52 >
< 11
10 >
< 9
8 >
< 7
6 >
< 5
4 >
< 3
2 >
< 1

rep for patt

8 sts to 12 sts to 8 sts

Reduced Front Basketweave Pattern

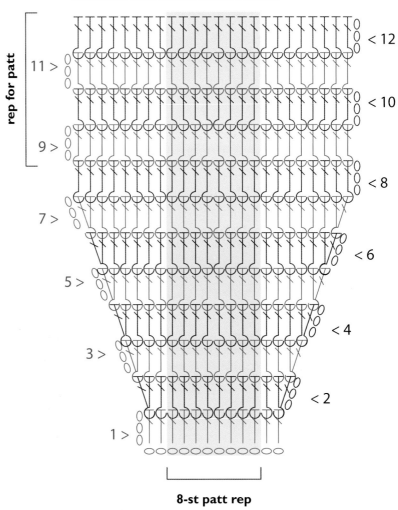

rep for patt

11 >
< 12
< 10
9 >
< 8
7 >
< 6
5 >
< 4
3 >
< 2
1 >

8-st patt rep

Stitch Key

- ● = slip stitch (sl st)
- ○ = chain (ch)
- ⊺ = double crochet (dc)
- ⊺ = front post double crochet (FPdc)
- ⊺ = back post double crochet (BPdc)
- ⊺ = front post half double crochet (FPhdc)
- ⊺ = back post half double crochet (BPhdc)
- ✗ = front post single crochet (FPsc)
- ✗ = back post single crochet (BPsc)

Reduced Front Flap with Tab

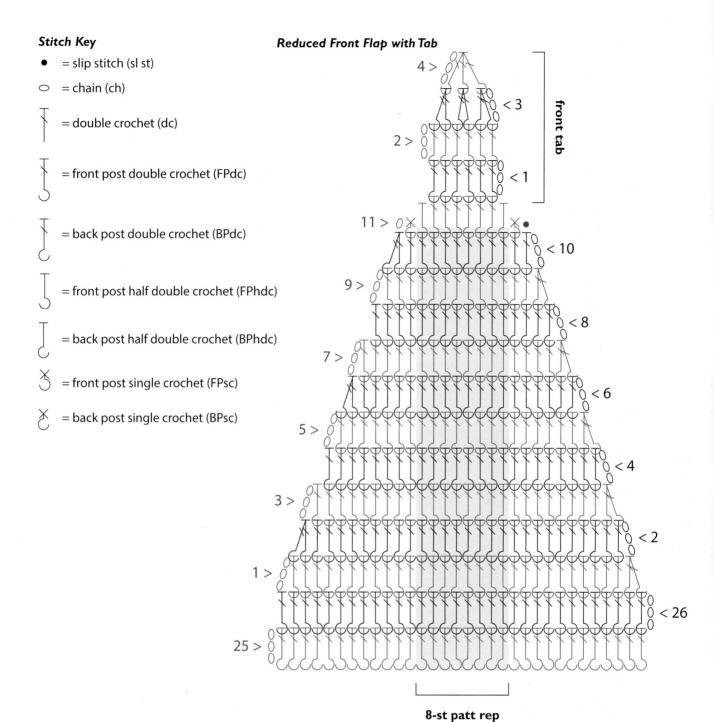

front tab

4 >
< 3
2 >
< 1

11 > < 10
9 >
< 8
7 >
< 6
5 >
< 4
3 >
< 2
1 >
< 26
25 >

8-st patt rep

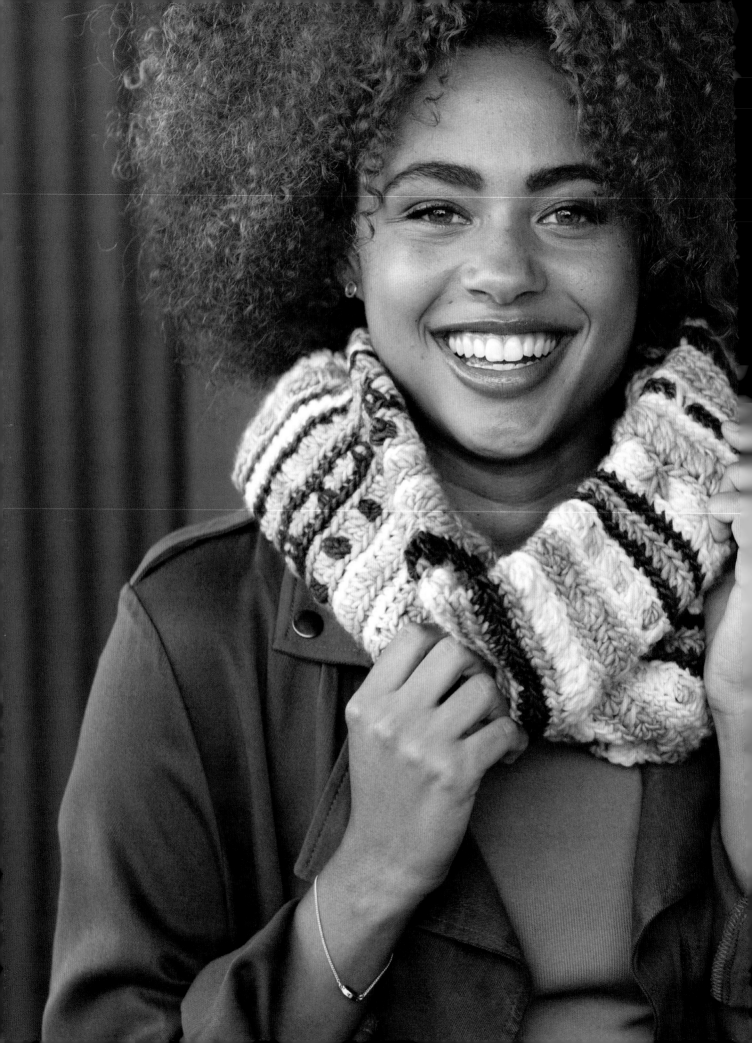

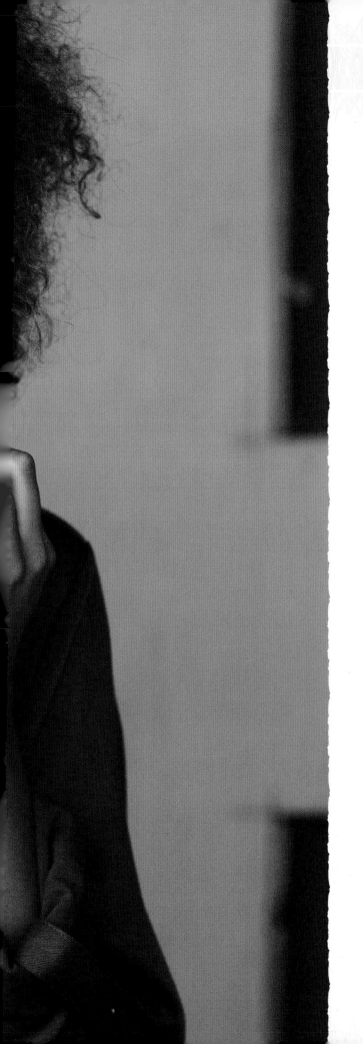

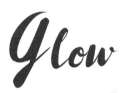

CHAPTER FOUR

Glow

Cozy on up to garments and accessories with serious warmth and sophisticated style. A bit of shimmer makes these projects perfect for the holidays, and bold patterns keep the frigid landscape colorful and bright. Make one for yourself and one to give away.

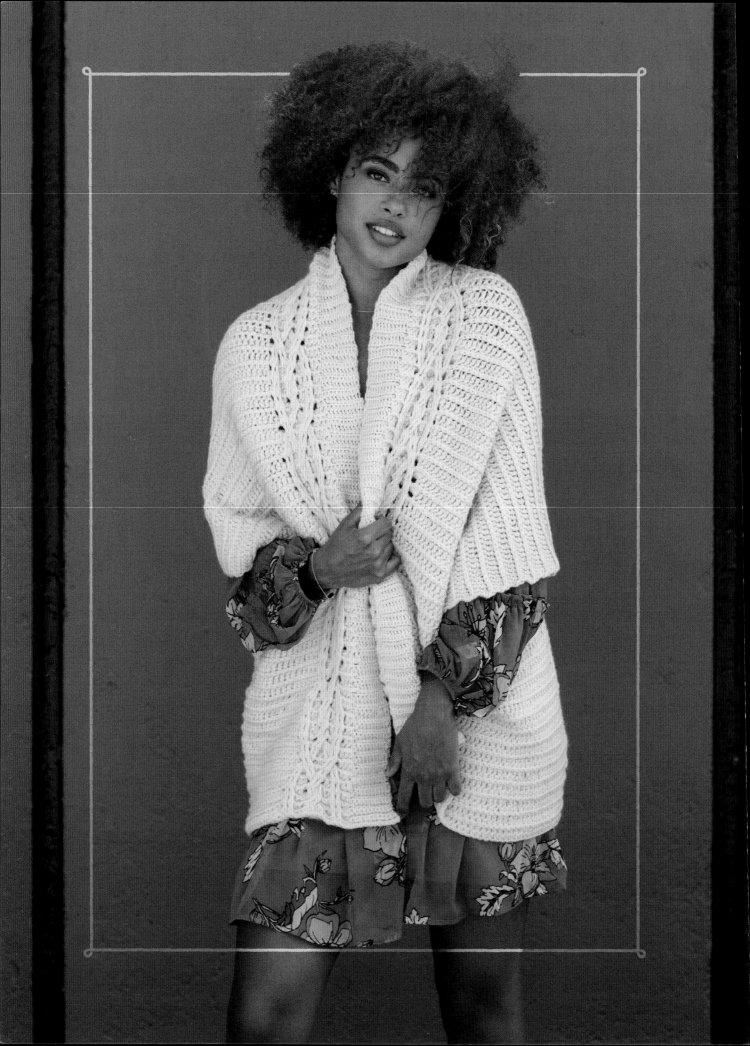

taylor cable cocoon

The silhouette of this sweater couldn't be simpler, but it's the cable detail that's the real feature. This cozy cocoon is inspired by an old pilled sweater a friend gave me that quickly became my favorite. I've made a few modifications to it, but the basic idea is the same. Working in the horizontal bar creates a lovely ribbed pattern on the fabric, and the cable keeps the work engaging.

FINISHED SIZE
17 (20, 21)" (43 [51, 53.5] cm) across back.

Cocoon shown measures 17" (43 cm).

YARN
Worsted weight (#4 Medium).

Shown here: Lion Brand Fisherman's Wool (100% wool; 465 yd [425 m]/8 oz [227 g]): #098 natural, 3 (4, 4) skeins.

HOOK
Size K/10½ (6.5 mm).

Adjust hook size if necessary to obtain correct gauge.

NOTIONS
Tapestry needle.

GAUGE
14 hdc and 11 rows = 4" (10 cm) working in horizontal bar on WS rows.

NOTES
Piece has natural bias that will straighten out during blocking. Check your stitch count from time to time.

Skip the stitches behind the post stitches unless otherwise noted.

Cocoon

RIGHT FRONT

Ch 68.

Row 1: (RS) Working in back bump of ch, sc in 2nd ch from hook and in next 9 ch, hdc in rem ch across, turn—10 front edge sc, 57 hdc.

Row 2: (WS) Ch 2, hdc in horizontal bar of each hdc across, sc blo in each sc, turn.

Row 3: Ch 1, sc blo in next 10 sc, hdc in first 2 hdc, FPdc around next 2 hdc, hdc in next 2 hdc, FPdc around next 4 dc, hdc in next 2 hdc, FPdc around next 2 hdc, hdc in each hdc across, turn.

Row 4 and all foll WS rows: Ch 2, hdc in horizontal bar of each hdc and FPdc across, sc blo in each sc, turn.

Row 5: Ch 1, sc blo in next 10 sc, hdc in first 2 hdc, FPdc around next 2 FPdc 2 rows below, hdc in next 2 hdc, sk next 2 FPdc 2 rows below, FPdc around next 2 FPdc 2 rows below, working behind sts just made, FPdc around 2 skipped FPdc 2 rows below, hdc in next 2 hdc, FPdc around next 2 FPdc 2 rows below, hdc in each hdc across, turn.

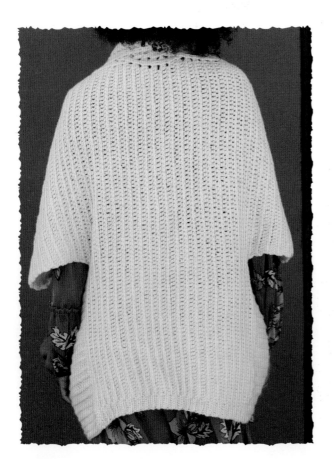

Row 7: Ch 1, sc blo in next 10 sc, hdc in first 2 hdc, FPdc around next 2 FPdc 2 rows below, hdc in next 2 hdc, FPdc around next 4 FPdc 2 rows below, hdc in next 2 hdc, FPdc around next 2 FPdc 2 rows below, hdc in each hdc across, turn.

Row 9: Rep Row 5.

Row 11: Ch 1, sc blo in next 10 sc, hdc in first 3 hdc, [FPdc around next 4 FPdc 2 rows below, hdc in next 2 hdc] twice, hdc in each hdc across, turn.

Row 13: Ch 1, sc blo in next 10 sc, hdc in first 3 hdc, *sk next 2 FPdc 2 rows below, FPdc around next 2 FPdc 2 rows below, working behind sts just made, FPdc around 2 skipped FPdc 2 rows below, hdc in next 2 hdc; rep from * once but work FPdc around 2 skipped FPdc in front of sts just made, hdc in each hdc across, turn.

Rows 15 and 17: Rep Row 5.

Rep Rows 7–18 until piece measures 27 (28, 29)" (68.5 [71, 73.5] cm), ending with a WS row.

BACK

Next row: (RS) Work in patt as established across, ch 43, turn.

Next row: Sc in 2nd ch from hook and in next 5 ch, hdc in next 36 ch, then cont in patt across, turn—10 front edge sc, 93 hdc, 6 back bottom sc.

Cont in patt until back measures 17 (20, 21)" (43 [51, 53.5] cm), ending with a WS row.

LEFT FRONT

Next row: (RS) Work in patt to last 36 hdc, turn, leaving rem hdc and sc unworked—10 front edge sc, 57 hdc rem.

Cont in patt until left front measures 27 (28, 29)" (68.5 [71, 73.5] cm) from back, ending with a WS row.

Last row: (RS) Ch 1, sc in next 10 sc, hdc in each hdc across. Fasten off.

Finishing

Wet-block, pin to measurements, let dry.

Fold right front to match up corners marked with X (see schematic). Using whipstitch, sew side seam, leaving a 16 (17, 18)" (40.5 [43, 45.5] cm) armhole. Fold left front to match up corners marked with Y. Sew as for right front. Weave in ends.

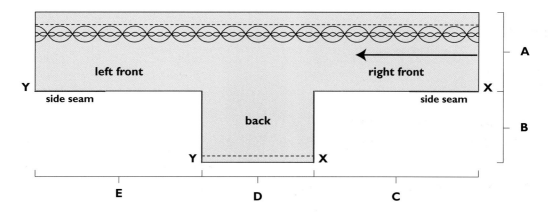

MEASUREMENTS

A: Front width
17¾" (45 cm)

B: Back length
11¼" (28.5 cm)

C: Right front length
27 (28, 29)" (68.5 [71, 73.5] cm)

D: Back width
17 (20, 21)" (43 [51, 53.5] cm)

E: Left front length
27 (28, 29)" (68.5 [71, 73.5] cm)

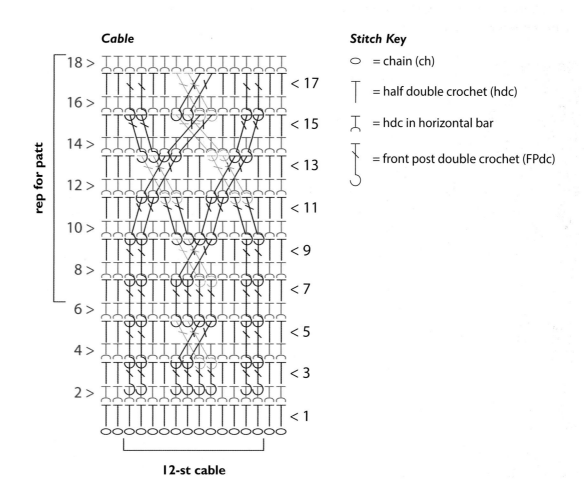

Cable

rep for patt

18 >
< 17
16 >
< 15
14 >
< 13
12 >
< 11
10 >
< 9
8 >
< 7
6 >
< 5
4 >
< 3
2 >
< 1

12-st cable

Stitch Key

◯ = chain (ch)

⊤ = half double crochet (hdc)

⟂ = hdc in horizontal bar

= front post double crochet (FPdc)

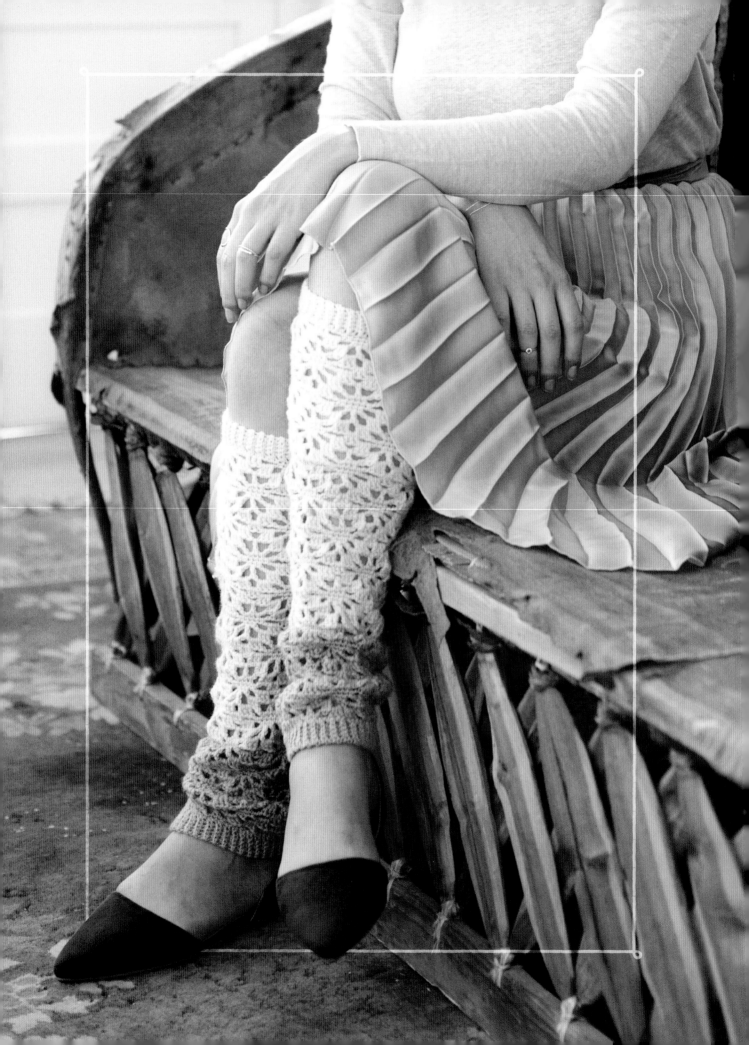

neva leg warmers

These leg warmers look more complicated than they are! The stitch pattern is quick to memorize, and simple color changes create an ombré effect. These would be cool peeking out over a pair of tall boots, or flip them over to match a different outfit. This is an easy, gratifying project.

FINISHED SIZE
About 11" (28 cm) in circumference and 16" (40.5 cm) long. To be worn with negative ease.

YARN
Sportweight (#2 Fine).

Shown here: Willow Yarns Attire Light (100% superwash extrafine merino; 143 yd [130 m]/1¾ oz [50 g]): #0001 snow (A), #0004 dove (B), and #0005 kitten (C), 1 skein each.

HOOK
Size F/5 (3.75 mm).

Adjust hook size if necessary to obtain correct gauge.

NOTIONS
Tapestry needle.

GAUGE
First 10 rows of main pattern create a circular piece 3" (7.5 cm) tall and 11" (28 cm) in circumference.

Leg Warmer (Make 2)

TOP RIBBING
With A, ch 6, turn.

Row 1: Sc in 2nd ch from hook and in each ch across, turn—5 sc.

Row 2: Ch 1, sc in blo of each sc across, turn.

Rows 3–70: Rep Row 2.

Sl st tog last row and first row to form a ring, taking care not to twist the ribbing, rotate piece to work in row-ends in the rnd.

LEG
Rnd 1: (RS) Ch 1, sc in each row-end around, sl st in first sc to join—70 sc.

Rnd 2: Ch 3 (counts as dc throughout), sk first sc, dc in next 2 sc, *ch 3, sk next 3 sc, sc in next 5 sc, ch 3, sk next 3 sc**, dc in next 3 sc; rep from * around, ending last rep at **, sl st in top of beg ch-3 to join.

Rnd 3: Sl st in next 2 dc, sl st in next ch-3 sp, ch 3 (counts as dc), 2 dc in same ch-3 sp, ch 3, *sk next sc, sc in next 3 sc, ch 3, 3 dc in next ch-3 sp, ch 1**, 3 dc in next ch-3 sp, ch 3; rep from * around, ending last rep at **, sl st in top of beg ch-3 to join.

Rnd 4: Sl st in next 2 dc, sl st in next ch-3 sp, ch 3 (counts as dc), 2 dc in same ch-3 sp, *ch 3, sk next sc, dc in next sc, ch 3, 3 dc in next ch-3 sp, ch 3, dc in next ch-1 sp, ch 3**, 3 dc in next ch-3 sp; rep from * around, ending last rep at**, sl st in top of beg ch-3 to join.

Rnd 5: Sl st in next 2 dc, sl st in next ch-3 sp, ch 3 (counts as dc), 2 dc in same ch-3 sp, *ch 1, 3 dc in next ch-3 sp, ch 3, sc in next ch-3 sp, sc in next dc, sc in next ch-3 sp, ch 3**, 3 dc in next ch-3 sp; rep from * around, ending last rep at **, sl st in top of beg ch-3 to join.

Rnd 6: Sl st in next 2 dc, sl st in next ch-1 sp, ch 3 (counts as dc), 2 dc in same sp, *ch 3, sc in next ch-3 sp, sc in next 3 sc, sc in next ch-3 sp, ch 3**, 3 dc in next ch-1 sp; rep from * around, ending last rep at **, sl st in top of beg ch-3 to join.

Rnds 7–14: Rep Rnds 3–6 twice.

Rnds 15–17: Rep Rnds 3–5. Fasten off A.

Rnd 18: Change to B, rep Rnd 6.

Rnds 19–34: Cont with B, rep Rnds 3–6 four times.

Rnds 35–37: Rep Rnds 3–5. Fasten off B.

Rnd 38: Change to C, rep Rnd 6.

Rnds 39–50: Cont with C, rep Rnds 3–6 three times.

Rnds 51–53: Rep Rnds 3–5. Fasten off.

BOTTOM RIBBING
With C, work as for top ribbing, but after you sl st ends tog to form a ring, fasten off, leaving a 30" (76 cm) tail. Using tapestry needle, sew bottom ribbing to top edge of Rnd 53 of leg.

Finishing
Weave in ends, block (wet or steam), and let dry.

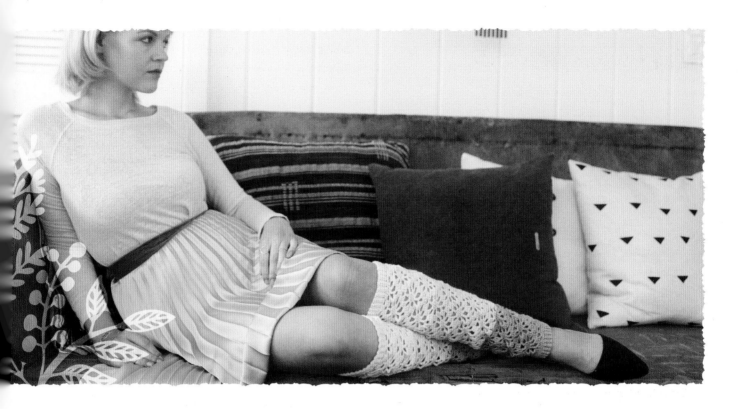

Main Pattern

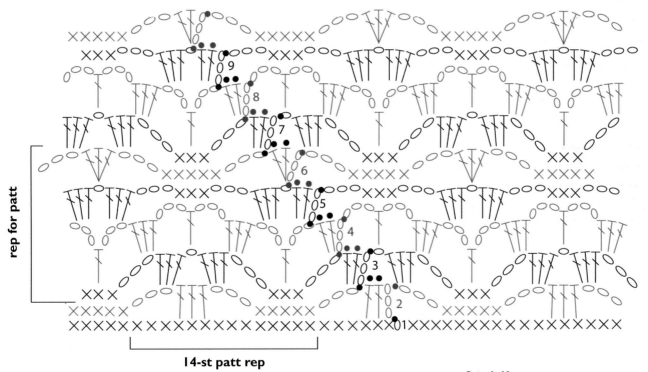

rep for patt

14-st patt rep

Stitch Key

● = slip stitch (sl st)

○ = chain (ch)

✕ = single crochet (sc)

⊤ = double crochet (dc)

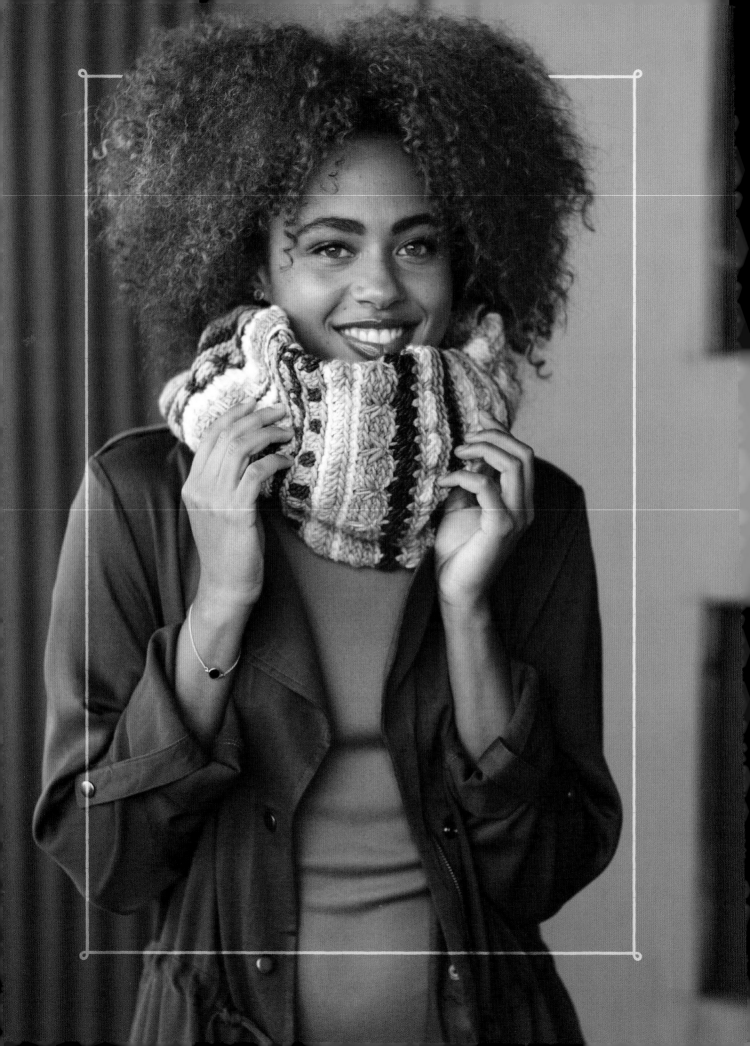

nordica cowl

Inspired by Fair Isle knitting, the Nordica Cowl features beautiful crochet colorwork and extravagant texture. A lofty one-ply yarn, such as Malabrigo Merino Worsted, provides warmth and body for this cozy accessory. The cowl is crocheted in the round in a tube shape, so there's no wrong side.

FINISHED SIZE
27" (68.5 cm) circumference and 10" (25.5 cm) tall.

YARN
Worsted weight (#4 Medium).

Shown here: Malabrigo Merino Worsted (100% merino wool; 210 yd [192 m]/3½ oz [100 g]): #MM063 natural (A), #MM069 pearl ten (dark purple; B), #MM601 simply taupe (C), and #MM009 polar morn (light blue; D), 1 skein each.

HOOK
Size I/9 (5.5 mm).

Adjust hook size if necessary to obtain correct gauge.

NOTIONS
Marker (optional); tapestry needle.

GAUGE
16 hdc = 4" (10 cm) wide and 20 rows (1 rep) = 6¾" (17 cm) tall.

NOTES
This cowl is worked in joined rounds, right side always showing.

Do not fasten off yarn at each color change; instead, carry colors that aren't currently used up the wrong side of the fabric.

STITCH GUIDE

FOUNDATION SINGLE CROCHET (FSC)
Start with a slipknot on hook, chain 2, insert hook in 2nd chain from hook, pull up lp, yarn over, draw through 1 lp (the "chain"), yarn over and draw through 2 lps (the single crochet), 1 sc with its own ch st at the bottom, *insert hook under 2 lps of the "ch" st of last st and pull up lp, yarn over and draw through 1 lp, yarn over and draw through 2 lps, repeat from * for length of foundation chain.

SPIKE
Insert hook in st 2 rows below and work an sc.

CLUSTER (CL)
Dc3tog in indicated st or sp. If rnd uses 2 colors, use contrasting color for last yo of cl to draw through all lps.

STAR
Insert hook in bottom of sc 1 row below and 1 st to the right, pull up a lp, insert hook in bottom of sc 2 rows below and 2 sts to the right, pull up a lp, insert hook in bottom of sc 3 rows below, pull up a lp, insert hook in bottom of sc 2 rows below and 2 sts to the left, pull up a lp, insert hook in bottom of sc 1 row below and 1 st to the left, pull up a lp (6 lps on hook), yo, draw through all lps on hook. Sk current st behind the star.

Cowl

Rnd 1: With A, leaving a long tail for sewing, work 80 fsc (see Stitch Guide), sl st in first sc to join, place marker if desired—80 sts. Do not turn and do not fasten off.

Rnd 2: Join B with sl st in first st, ch 2 (counts as hdc throughout), sk first st, hdc blo in each sc around, sl st in top of beg ch-2 to join.

Rnd 3: Change to A, ch 1, sc in top of beg ch-2, sc blo in next 2 hdc, spike (see Stitch Guide), *sc blo in next 3 hdc, spike; rep from * around, sl st in first sc to join.

Rnd 4: Join C with sl st in first st, ch 1, sc blo in same st and in each st around, sl st in first sc to join.

Rnd 5: With C, ch 3 (counts as dc throughout), sk first sc, dc blo in next 2 sc, with A, cl (see Stitch Guide) blo in next st, *with C, dc blo in next 3 sc, with A, cl blo in next sc; rep from * around, sl st in top of beg ch-3 to join.

Rnd 6: Join D with sl st in first st, ch 1, sc in top of beg ch-3, sc blo in each st around, sl st in first sc to join.

Rnd 7: With B, ch 2, sk first sc, hdc blo in each sc around, sl st in top of beg ch-2 to join.

Rnd 8: With D, ch 1, sc in top of beg ch-2, sc blo in each hdc around, sl st in first sc to join.

Rnds 9–11: With C, ch 1, sc blo in same st and in each st around, sl st in first sc to join.

Rnd 12: With B, ch 1, sc blo in same st and in next 3 sc, star (see Stitch Guide), *sc blo in next 4 sc, star; rep from * around, sl st in first sc to join—16 stars.

Rnd 13: With A, ch 3, dc2tog blo in same st, ch 1, sk next st, *cl blo in next st, ch 1, sk next st; rep from * around, sl st in top of beg ch-3 to join.

Rnd 14: With C, ch 1, sc blo in each cl and ch-1 sp around, sl st in first sc to join.

Rnd 15: With D, ch 2, sk first sc, hdc blo in each sc around, sl st in top of beg ch-2 to join.

Rnd 16: With C, ch 1, sc in top of beg ch-2, sc blo in next 2 hdc, spike in next 2 hdc, *sc blo in next 3 hdc, spike in next 2 hdc; rep from * around, sl st in first sc to join.

Rnd 17: With B, ch 1, sc blo in same st and in each st around, sl st in first sc to join.

Rnd 18: With A, ch 2, sk first sc, hdc blo in each sc around, sl st in top of beg ch-2 to join.

Rnd 19: With B, ch 1, sc in top of beg ch-2, sc blo in each hdc around, sl st in first sc to join.

Rnd 20: With D, ch 3, dc2tog blo in same st, ch 1, sk next st, *cl blo in next st, ch 1, sk next st; rep from * around, sl st in top of beg ch-3 to join.

Rnds 21–40: Rep Rnds 1–20, working Rnd 1 as sc blo not fsc, substituting colors as foll: work B in place of A, C in place of B, D in place of C, and A in place of D.

Rnds 41–60: Rep Rnds 1–20, working Rnd 1 as sc blo not fsc, substituting colors as foll: with C in place of A, D in place of B, A in place of C, and B in place of D.

Rnds 61–80: Rep Rnds 1–20, working Rnd 1 as sc blo not fsc, substituting colors as foll: with D in place of A, A in place of B, B in place of C, and C in place of D. Fasten off.

Assembly

Weave in ends except beginning long one. Steam block gently. Using whipstitch and long tail, sew last round to first round and weave in end.

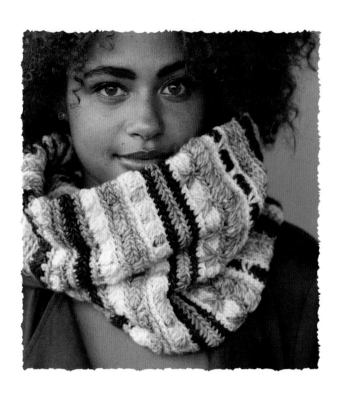

Colorwork

rep for patt

< 19
< 17
< 15
< 13
< 11
< 9
< 7
< 5
< 3
< 1

20-st patt rep

Stitch Key

⌒ = back loop only (blo)

o = chain (ch)

✕ = single crochet (sc)

⤫ = foundation chain (fsc)

T = half double crochet (hdc)

† = double crochet (dc)

⋁ = spike

⬮ = cluster (cl)

⋀ = star

▬ = work with A

▬ = work with B

▬ = work with C

▬ = work with D

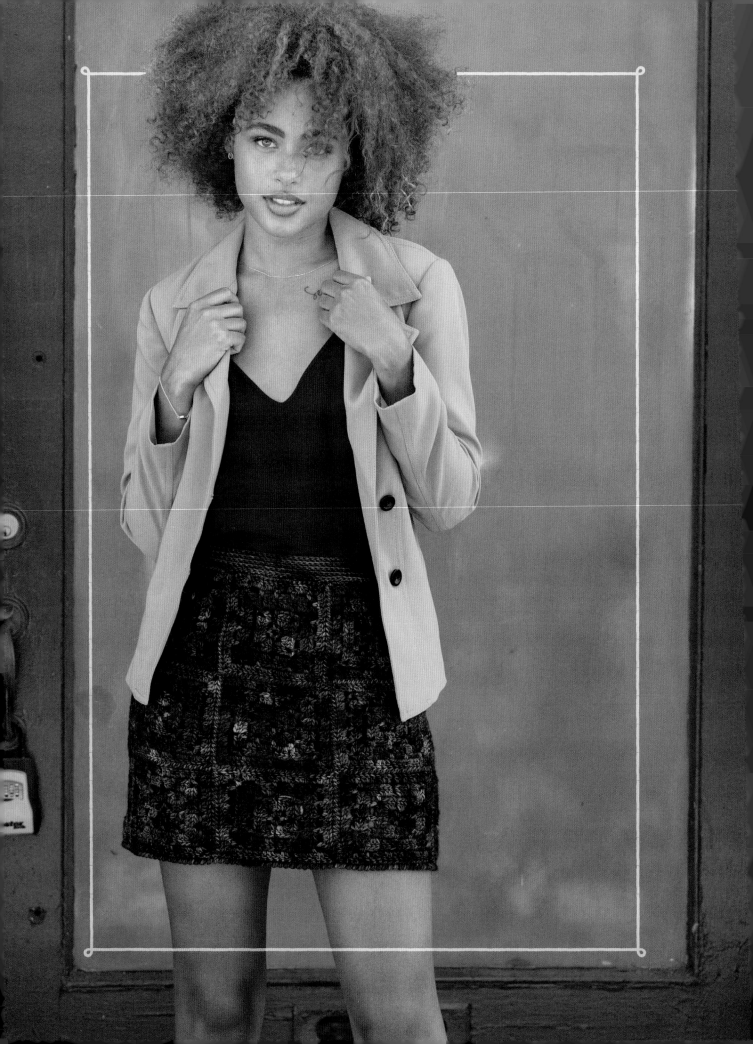

christiana skirt

This isn't your typical granny-square skirt. Worked in two similar colors, it has a sophisticated monochromatic look. The squares are easy to work and quick to memorize, so even a beginner could pull this look off. I love to use vintage buttons for projects like these—it's a great place to showcase some little treasures.

FINISHED SIZE
About 25¼ (28¾, 32¼, 35¾, 39½)" (64 [73, 82, 90.5, 100.5] cm) waist circumference, buttoned; 16½" (42 cm) long.

Skirt shown measures 25¼" (64 cm).

YARN
Worsted weight (#4 Medium).

Shown here: Malabrigo Merino Worsted (100% merino wool; 210 yd [192 m]/3½ oz [100 g]): #MM069 pearl ten (variegated purple; A) and #MM118 tortuga (dark charcoal; B), 2 (2, 3, 3, 4) skeins each.

HOOK
Size H/8 (5 mm).

Adjust hook size if necessary to obtain correct gauge.

NOTIONS
Tapestry needle; six ½" (1.3 cm) buttons; ½ (½, 1, 1, 1) yd (45.5 [45.5, 91.5, 91.5, 91.5] cm] knit fabric for lining; sewing needle and thread.

GAUGE
One granny square = 5" (12.5 cm) square.

NOTES
To have fewer ends to weave in at the end, crochet over the ends as you go. Simply lay yarn tails along top edge of previous row and work stitches over them to encase them.

To adjust waist circumference, work fewer or more stitches between decreases.

Skirt

SQUARE

With A, ch 4, sl st in first ch to form a ring.

Rnd 1: Ch 1, [sc in ring, ch 3] 4 times, sl st in first sc to join—4 ch-3 sps.

Rnd 2: Sk first sc, sl st in next ch-3 sp, ch 3 (counts as dc), (2 dc, ch 3, 3 dc) in same ch-3 sp, [(3 dc, ch 3, 3 dc) in next ch-3 sp] 3 times, sl st in top of beg ch-3 to join—4 ch-3 corners. Fasten off.

Rnd 3: Join B with sl st in any ch-3 corner sp, ch 1, (sc, ch 3, sc) in same sp, *ch 3, sk next 3 dc, sc bet dc-groups, ch 3**, (sc, ch 3, sc) in next ch-3 corner sp; rep from * around, ending last rep at **, sl st in first sc to join.

Rnd 4: Sl st in ch-3 corner sp, ch 3 (counts as dc), (2 dc, ch 3, 3 dc) in same sp, *3 dc in next 2 ch-3 sps**, (3 dc, ch 3, 3 dc) in next ch-3 corner sp; rep from * around, ending last rep at **, sl st in top of beg ch-3 to join. Fasten off.

Rnd 5: Join A with sl st in any ch-3 corner sp, (sc, ch 3, sc) in same sp, *[ch 3, sk next 3 dc, sc bet next dc-groups] 3 times, ch 3**, (sc, ch 3, sc) in next ch-3 corner sp; rep from * around, ending last rep at **, sl st in first sc to join.

Rnd 6: Sl st in ch-3 corner sp, ch 3 (counts as dc), (2 dc, ch 3, 3 dc) in same sp, *3 dc in next 4 ch-3 sps**, (3 dc, ch 3, 3 dc) in next ch-3 corner sp; rep from * around, ending last rep at **, sl st in top of beg ch-3 to join. Fasten off.

Make 10 (12, 13, 15, 16) squares with this color scheme, then make 11 (12, 14, 15, 17) squares starting with B, switching to A, and then finishing with B.

ASSEMBLY

With RS facing, arrange the squares in 3 rows and 7 (8, 9, 10, 11) columns in a color pattern you like or alternate differently colored squares for rows and columns. For an odd number of columns, the first and last column will be the same. With lighter color of yarn and needle, whipstitch squares together, or use your favorite method of joining granny squares, to form a large rectangle. I like sewing them rather than sc them together because I like for the joints to be more subtle, but do whatever you prefer. At this point, lay the rectangle out on your lining fabric and cut your lining, remembering to add ½" (1.3 cm) for seam allowance at each side. You don't need seam allowance at the top and the bottom. Now join the rectangle into a tube and sew from the bottom up for 2 rows of squares, leaving the top square open for the button placket.

Finishing

WAISTBAND

With RS facing, join lighter yarn in top right ch-3 corner sp.

Row 1: (RS) Ch 1, sc in same sp, *sc in each dc across top of square, sc in corner sp**, sc in corner sp of next square; rep from * around, ending last rep at **, turn—140 (160, 180, 200, 220) sc.

Row 2 (dec): Ch 1, working in the back lp only, sc in first 3 sc, sc2tog, *sc in next 3 sc, sc2tog (see Notes); rep from * around, turn—112 (128, 144, 160, 176) sc rem.

Rows 3 and 4: Ch 1, sc blo in each sc around, turn.

BUTTON PLACKET

Row 5: (RS) Ch 1, sc blo in each sc around, at the end of the row work 3 sc in the corner, then work 24 sc evenly down along opening to seam, sl st in side seam, turn.

Row 6 (short-row): Sc in each sc up placket side, stopping at top of waistband, turn.

Row 7 (short-row): Ch 1, sc in each sc down placket side, sl st in last sc, turn.

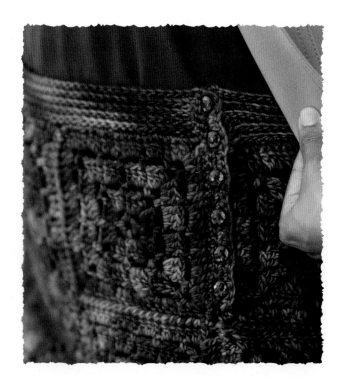

Row 8: Sc in each sc up placket side to top of waistband, 3 sc in corner, turn piece to work back along the waistband, sc blo in each sc around waistband.

Rows 9–11: Rep Row 3.

Row 12: (WS) Ch 1, sc blo in each sc around, at the end of the row, work 3 sc in the corner, then work 24 sc evenly down along opening to seam, sl st in side seam, turn.

Row 13 (buttonholes): Sc in first 2 sc, [ch 1, sk next sc, sc in next 3 sc] 5 times, sc in last 2 sc, turn.

Row 14: Ch 1, sc in each sc and ch-1 sp down opening edge, sl st in side seam. Fasten off.

HEM EDGING

With RS facing, join darker yarn anywhere along hem edge.

Rnd 1: Ch 1, sc in each sc and corner sp around, sl st in first sc to join.

Rnd 2: Ch 1, rsc in each sc around, sl st in first sc to join. Fasten off.

Weave in ends. Steam block gently. Using needle and thread, sew buttons to button placket opposite buttonholes. Seam lining. Fold bottom edge to same side as seam allowance and sew ¼" (6 mm) from folded edge around. Repeat for top edge. Sew lining with WS facing skirt into skirt to hide seam allowances.

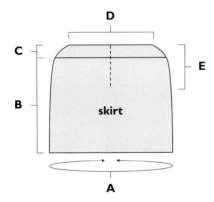

MEASUREMENTS

A: Hip circumference
35 (40, 45, 50, 55)" (89 [101.5, 114.5, 127, 139.5] cm)

B: Skirt length to waistband
15¼" (38.5 cm)

C: Waistband height
1½" (3.8 cm)

D: Waist circumference
25 (28¾, 32¼, 35¾, 39¼)" (63.5 [73, 82, 90.5, 99.5] cm)

E: Button placket length
6½" (16.5 cm)

Square

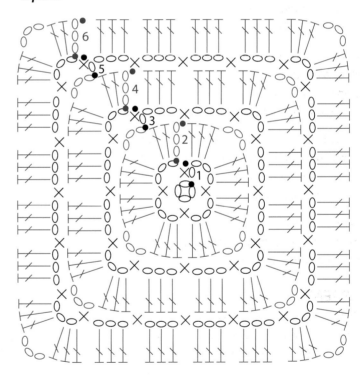

Stitch Key

● = slip stitch (sl st)

○ = chain (ch)

✕ = single crochet (sc)

† = double crochet (dc)

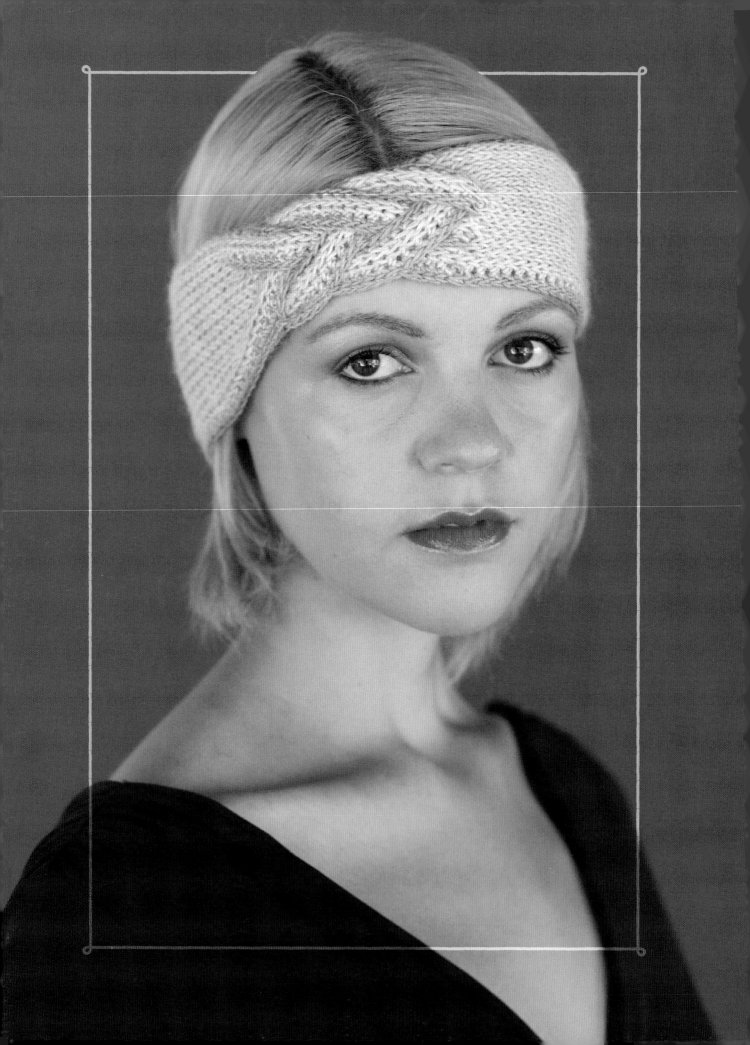

luna headband

This headband and the following hat were inspired by chic turban-style headbands. I love to incorporate braiding into my patterns because it looks intricate, but it's actually simple. If you've never braided with five strands before, it's just as easy as braiding with three.

FINISHED SIZE
18½" (47 cm) long and 3" (7.5 cm) wide.

Fits up to 23" (58.5 cm) head circumference.

YARN
Sportweight (#2 Fine).

Shown here: Blue Sky Fibers Metalico (50% baby alpaca, 50% raw silk; 147 yd [135 m]/1¾ oz [50 g]): #1611 silver (MC), 1 skein; #1613 gold dust (CC), 1 skein.

HOOK
Size H/8 (5 mm) Tunisian hook.

Adjust hook size if necessary to obtain correct gauge.

NOTIONS
Tapestry needle; pins (optional); one ½" (1.3 cm) button (more if you want to make headband adjustable).

GAUGE
20 sts and 25 rows = 4" (10 cm) in Tunisian knit stitch.

NOTES
CC optional because you'll need only a few yards of it for the edging. You can work the whole headband in MC if desired.

To make headband adjustable, place more than 1 button in a row at one end, then pick which button to place button lp around.

STITCH GUIDE

INCREASE (INC)
Draw up a lp bet 2 sts—1 st inc'd.

DECREASE (DEC)
Insert hook through 2 sts instead of 1 and draw up a lp—1 st dec'd.

Headband

With MC, ch 3.

Row 1: FwP: Draw up lp in each ch across—4 lps on hook. RetP: Yo, draw through first lp on hook, *yo, draw through next 2 lps; rep from * across row. Use this return pass for every row.

Row 2 (inc): FwP: Working in TKS, work inc (see Stitch Guide) (drawing up lp bet first and 2nd st), then draw up lp in each st across to last st, inc. RetP—2 sts inc'd.

Rows 3–7: Rep Row 2—14 sts at end of Row 7.

Row 8 (inc): Inc, TKS in each st across—15 sts. RetP.

Cont even in TKS until piece measures 9½" (24 cm) from beg.

BRAID STRANDS

Strand 1: Pull up lps in the first 2 sts (3 lps on hook), leaving rem sts unworked. Work in TKS across these 3 sts for 22 rows. Fasten off.

Center strands: Join yarn in base next to last st of strand 1, pull up lps in next 9 sts (9 lps on hook), leaving rem 3 sts unworked. Work in TKS across these 9 sts for 3 rows.

Strand 2: Pull up lps in first 2 sts (3 lps on hook), leaving rem sts unworked. Work in TKS across these 3 sts for 19 rows. Fasten off.

Strand 3: Join yarn in base next to last st of strand 2, pull up lps in next 3 sts, leaving last 3 sts unworked. Work in TKS across these 3 sts for 19 rows. Fasten off.

Strand 4: Join yarn in base next to last st of strand 3, pull up lps in last 3 sts. Work in TKS across these 3 sts for 19 rows. Fasten off.

Strand 5: Join yarn in base next to last st of center strands, pull up lps in last 3 sts. Work in TKS across these 3 sts for 22 rows. Fasten off.

STRAND EDGING
Edging can be worked in the same color or in a contrasting color.

Join CC with sl st in first st of strand 1, *sc in each row-end up along strand 1, at end, ch 3, sk the 3 sts, then sc in each row-end down other side of strand 1; rep from * for rem strands. Fasten off.

BRAIDING
With RS facing and strands at the top of the piece, numbered 1–5 from right to left, braid as foll:

Step 1: Pass rightmost strand to the left over next 2 strands to become new center strand.

Step 2: Pass leftmost strand to the right over next 2 strands to become new center strand.

Rep steps 1 and 2 two more times, pinning strands in place if needed. Braided strands will measure about 4" (10 cm) long.

BAND END
With RS facing, join MC in top right of first braided strand, draw up 3 lps across each strand of braided piece. RetP—15 sts.

Cont in TKS until piece measures 17" (43 cm) from beg.

Next row (dec): Working in TKS, dec (see Stitch Guide), then draw up lp in each st across to last 2 sts, dec. RetP—2 sts dec'd.

Rep last row 5 more times—3 sts rem.

Last row: (RS) Sc in each st across, ch 5, sl st in first sc of row for button loop. Fasten off.

Finishing

With RS facing, join CC in first st at beg of headband, ch 1, sc evenly in row-ends up along edge to braided strands, sl st in each st of strand edging facing the edge, then sc evenly in row-ends to button loop, sc in each ch of lp, sc evenly in row-ends down other side to braided strands, sl st in each st of strand edging facing the edge, then sc evenly in row-ends to bottom corner, sc in each st across to end, sl st in first sc to join. Fasten off.

Weave in ends. Steam block lightly. With RS facing, sew on button(s) at opposite end of button loop.

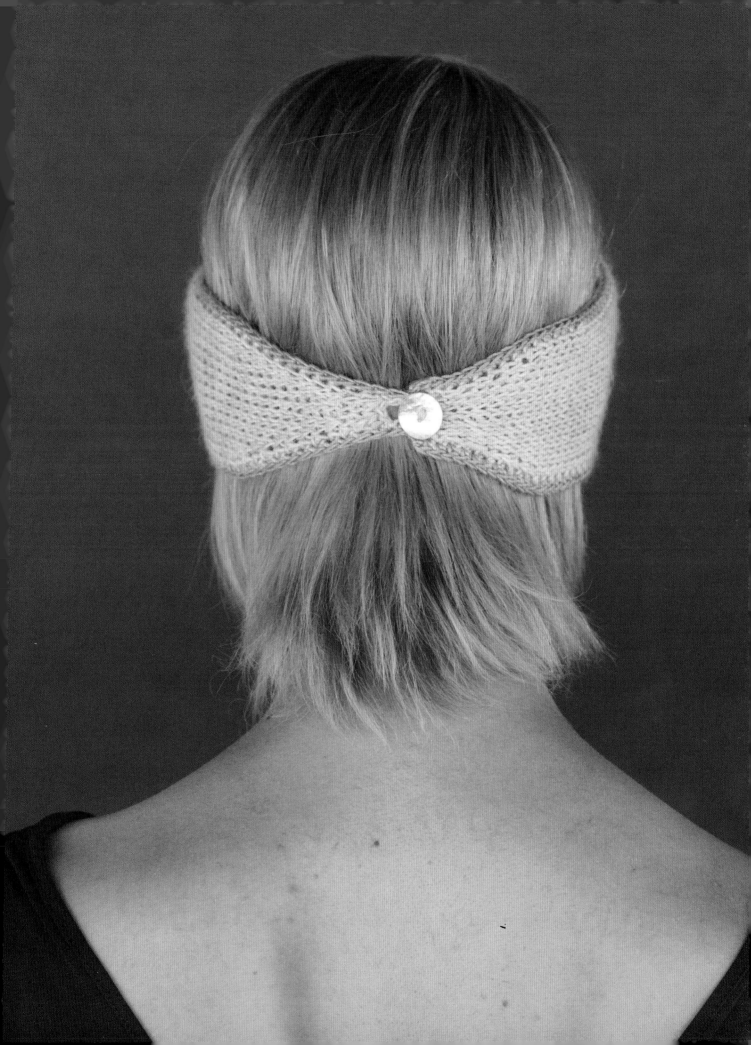

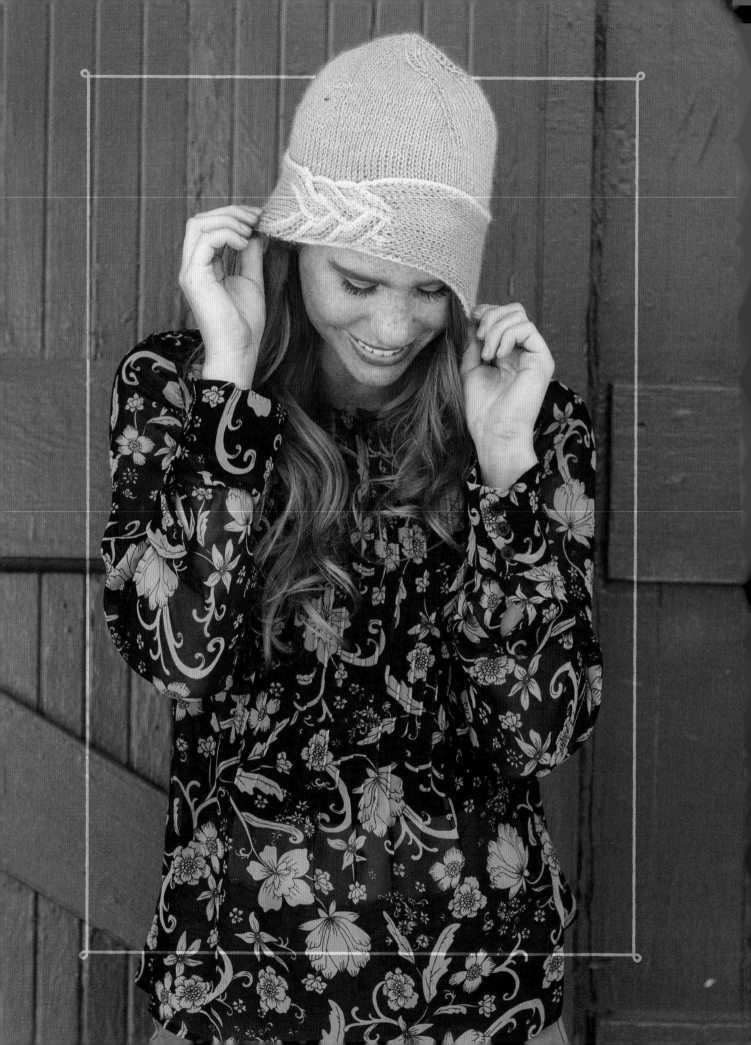

luna hat

This hat and the previous headband look exactly like a knitted project, but in this instance, Tunisian crochet provides a much warmer and sturdier fabric than knitting. Blue Sky Fibers Metalico provides a subtle metallic shimmer with all the softness you'd want in a winter hat.

FINISHED SIZE

18½" (47 cm) circumference and 8" (20.5 cm) tall.

Fits up to 23" (58.5 cm) head circumference.

YARN

Sportweight (#2 Fine).

Shown here: Blue Sky Fibers Metalico (50% baby alpaca, 50% raw silk; 147 yd [135 m]/1¾ oz [50 g]): #1613 gold dust (MC), 2 skeins; #1611 silver (CC), 1 skein.

HOOK

Size H/8 (5 mm) double-ended Tunisian hook.

Adjust hook size if necessary to obtain correct gauge.

NOTIONS

Tapestry needle; pins (optional); markers (m).

GAUGE

20 sts and 25 rows = 4" (10 cm) in Tunisian knit stitch.

NOTES

CC optional because you'll need only a few yards of it for the edging. You can work the whole hat in MC if desired.

STITCH GUIDE

DECREASE (DEC)
Insert hook through 2 sts instead of 1 and draw up a lp—1 st dec'd.

Hat

BAND
With MC, ch 14.

Row 1: FwP: Draw up lp in each ch across—15 lps on hook. RetP: Yo, draw through first lp on hook, *yo, draw through next 2 lps; rep from * across row. Use this return pass for every row.

Work in TKS until piece measures 9½" (24 cm). Work braid as for headband, then work even until piece measures 18½" (47 cm) from beg. Fasten off.

BAND EDGING
With tapestry needle and using mattress stitch, sew last row to first row forming a ring. With RS facing, join CC at seam, ch 1, work edging as for headband along top edge of band that will attach to hat. Fasten off.

BODY
Wind off MC for a 2nd ball of yarn for working the hat in Tunisian crochet in the round.

With double-ended Tunisian hook, join MC at seam. Place marker and move m up as you work.

Rnd 1: (RS) Draw up and work off 95 lps around top edge of band as foll: beg drawing up lps for about a third of the circumference by inserting the hook from the back to the front to the back around row-ends of band just below contrast edging, turn piece to wrong side, join 2nd ball of yarn and start working off lps with other end of the hook by beg with a yo, draw through 1 lp, then yo, draw through 2 lps until about 3 lps rem on hook, turn work back to right side, *cont with first ball of yarn and draw up lps around for the next third of the circumference, turn work to wrong side, with 2nd ball of yarn and other end of hook, yo and cont to draw through 2 lps until about 3 lps rem on hook, turn work and rep from * to end (about 3 lps rem on hook).

Rnd 2: Work in TKS around as established, always drawing yarn through 2 lps when working lps off hook.

Cont as established for 13 more rnds or until piece measures 5" (12.5 cm) from bottom edge of band.

CROWN
Rnd 16 (dec): [Work dec (see Stitch Guide), 17 TKS] 5 times—90 sts rem.

Rnd 17: Work even in TKS around.

Rnd 18: [Work dec, 16 TKS] 5 times—5 sts dec'd.

Rnds 19–27: Rep Rnds 17 and 18 four times, working 1 fewer st bet dec each rep, then work Rnd 17 once more—65 sts rem.

Rnds 28–38: Rep Rnd 18 eleven times, working 1 fewer st bet dec each rep—10 sts rem.

Next rnd: Work dec 5 times—5 sts rem.

Fasten off both yarns, leaving a 12" (30.5 cm) tail. Thread tails through rem sts, draw tight to close the hole, tie a knot, and weave in ends.

Finishing
With RS facing, join CC at seam of bottom band edge, ch 1, work edging as for headband. Fasten off.

Weave in ends. Steam block gently.

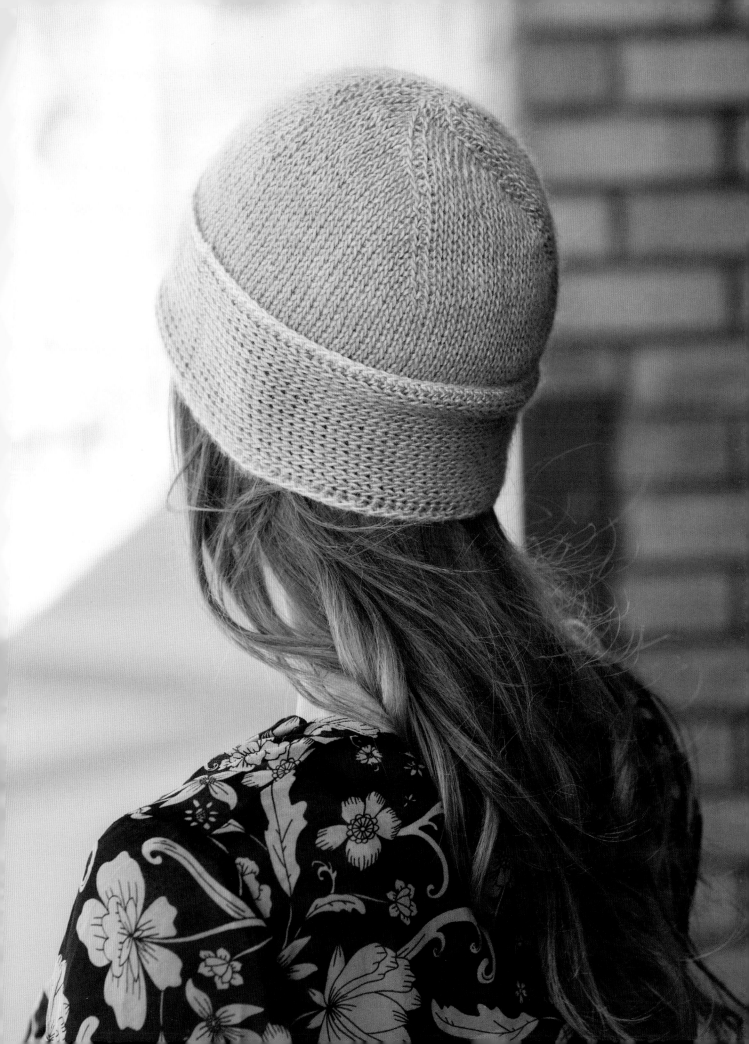

Abbreviations

beg	begin; begins; beginning	mm	millimeter(s)
bet	between	patt(s)	pattern(s)
blo	back loop only	pm	place marker
BPdc	back post double crochet	rem	remain(s); remaining
BPhdc	back post half double crochet	rep	repeat; repeating
BPsc	back post single crochet	RetP	return pass
BPtr	back post treble crochet	rnd(s)	round(s)
CC	contrasting color	RS	right side
ch(s)	chain(s)	rsc	reverse single crochet
cm	centimeter(s)	sc	single crochet
cont	continue(s); continuing	sc2tog	single crochet two together
dc	double crochet	sc3tog	single crochet three together
dc2tog	double crochet two together	sk	skip
dc3tog	double crochet three together	sl	slip
dec	decrease(s); decreasing	sl st	slip(ped) stitch
dec'd	decreased	sp(s)	space(s)
dtr	double treble crochet	st(s)	stitch(es)
flo	front loop only	tch	turning chain
foll	follows; following	TKS	Tunisian Knit Stitch
FPdc	front post double crochet	tog	together
FPhdc	front post half double crochet	tr	treble crochet
FPsc	front post single crochet	ttr	triple treble crochet
FPtr	front post treble crochet	WS	wrong side
fsc	foundation single crochet	yd	yard(s)
FwP	forward pass	yo	yarn over
g	gram(s)	*	repeat starting point
hdc	half double crochet	( )	alternative measurements and/or instructions; work instructions within parentheses in place directed
inc	increase(s); increasing		
inc'd	increased	[]	work bracketed instructions a specified number of times
lp(s)	loop(s)		
MC	main color		
m	marker; meter(s)		

Glossary
Stitches

CHAIN (CH)

Make a slipknot and place it on crochet hook. *Yarn over hook and draw through loop on hook. Repeat from * for the desired number of stitches.

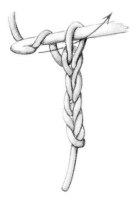

SLIP STITCH (SL ST)

*Insert hook in stitch, yarn over and draw loop through stitch and loop on hook; repeat from *.

SINGLE CROCHET (SC)

Insert hook into a stitch, yarn over hook and draw up a loop (Figure 1), yarn over hook and draw it through both loops on hook (Figure 2).

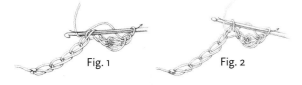

Fig. 1   Fig. 2

HALF DOUBLE CROCHET (HDC)

*Yarn over, insert hook in stitch (Figure 1), yarn over and pull up loop (3 loops on hook), yarn over (Figure 2) and draw through all loops on hook (Figure 3); repeat from *.

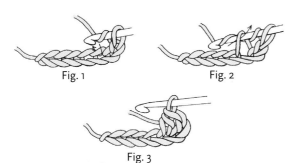

Fig. 1   Fig. 2

Fig. 3

DOUBLE CROCHET (DC)

*Yarn over hook, insert hook in a stitch, yarn over hook and draw up a loop (3 loops on hook; Figure 1), yarn over hook and draw it through 2 loops (Figure 2), yarn over hook and draw it through remaining 2 loops on hook (Figure 3). Repeat from *.

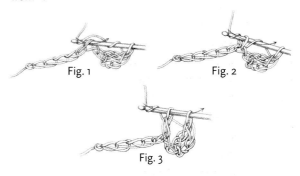

Fig. 1   Fig. 2

Fig. 3

TREBLE CROCHET (TR)

*Wrap yarn around hook twice, insert hook in next indicated stitch, yarn over hook and draw up a loop (4 loops on hook; Figure 1), yarn over hook and draw it through 2 loops (Figure 2), yarn over hook and draw it through next 2 loops, yarn over hook and draw it through the remaining 2 loops on hook (Figure 3). Repeat from *.

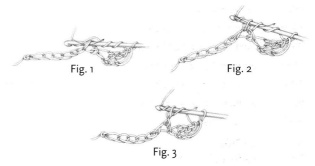

Fig. 1   Fig. 2

Fig. 3

DOUBLE TREBLE CROCHET (DTR)

Yarn over 3 times and insert hook in 6th chain from hook. Draw a loop through chain—5 loops on hook; [yarn over and draw through 2 loops] 4 times.

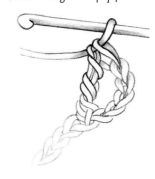

TRIPLE TREBLE CROCHET (TTR)

Yarn over 4 times, insert hook in stitch, yarn over and pull up loop (6 loops on hook), yarn over and draw through 2 loops 5 times.

REVERSE SINGLE CROCHET (RSC)

Working from left to right, insert crochet hook in an edge stitch and pull up loop, yarn over and draw this loop through the first one to join, *insert hook in next stitch to right (Figure 1), pull up a loop, yarn over (Figure 2), and draw through both loops on hook (Figure 3); repeat from *.

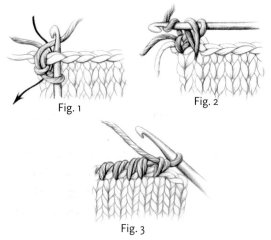

Fig. 1

Fig. 2

Fig. 3

FRONT POST DOUBLE CROCHET (FPDC)

Yarn over hook, insert hook from front to back to front again around post of stitch indicated, yarn over hook and pull up a loop (3 loops on hook), [yarn over hook and draw through 2 loops on hook] twice—1 FPdc made.

BACK POST SINGLE CROCHET (BPSC)

Insert hook from back to front to back around post of corresponding stitch below, yarn over and pull up loop, yarn over and draw through 2 loops on hook.

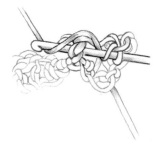

PICOT

Ch 3, sl st in first ch made.

TUNISIAN KNIT STITCH (TKS)

TKS forward pass (FwP): (lp on hook counts as first st) Sk first vertical bars, with yarn in back, *insert hook bet next

vertical bars under horizontal strands (**Figure 1**), yo and pull up lp, leave lp on hook; rep from * to last vertical bar at edge, draw up lp through the lp on the side of the work as well as the last vertical bar for a nice edge; return pass.

Return pass (RetP): Yo and draw lp through first lp on hook, *yo and draw through 2 lps on hook; rep from * across (**Figure 2**), ending with 1 lp on hook.

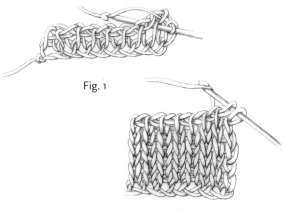

Fig. 1

Fig. 2

Decreases

SINGLE CROCHET TWO TOGETHER (SC2TOG)

Insert hook in stitch and draw up a loop. Insert hook in next stitch and draw up a loop. Yarn over hook (Figure 1). Draw through all 3 loops on hook (Figures 2 and 3)—1 stitch decreased.

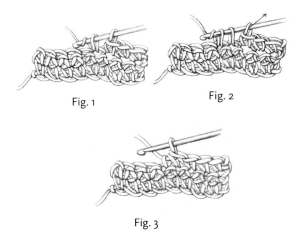

Fig. 1

Fig. 2

Fig. 3

SINGLE CROCHET THREE TOGETHER (SC3TOG)

[Insert hook in next stitch, yarn over, pull loop through stitch] 3 times (4 loops on hook). Yarn over and draw yarn through all 4 loops on hook. Completed sc3tog—2 stitches decreased.

DOUBLE CROCHET TWO TOGETHER (DC2TOG)

[Yarn over, insert hook in next stitch, yarn over and pull up loop (Figure 1), yarn over, draw through 2 loops] twice (Figure 2), yarn over, draw through all loops on hook (Figure 3)—1 stitch decreased (Figure 4).

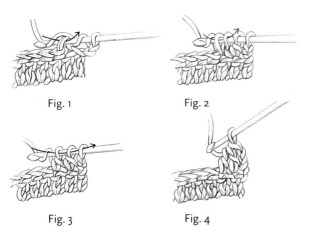

Fig. 1   Fig. 2

Fig. 3   Fig. 4

DOUBLE CROCHET THREE TOGETHER (DC3TOG)

[Yarn over, insert hook in next stitch, yarn over and pull up loop, yarn over, draw through 2 loops] 3 times (4 loops on hook), yarn over, draw through all loops on hook—2 stitches decreased.

Seaming

MATTRESS STITCH

Hold both pieces to be joined with the right sides facing and edges parallel to each other. Use threaded yarn needle to *insert the needle vertically under and out a stitch (or post) on the first piece and then under and out of the corresponding stitch (or post) of the second piece. Repeat from * to end of seam.

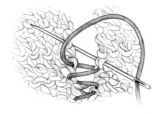 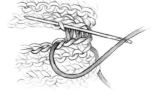

WHIPSTITCH

With right sides (RS) of work facing and working through edge stitches, bring threaded needle out from back to front, along edge of piece.

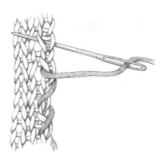

Blocking

STEAM BLOCKING

Pin the pieces to be blocked to a blocking surface. Hold an iron set on the steam setting ½" (1.3 cm) above the knitted surface and direct the steam over the entire surface (except ribbing). You can get similar results by lapping wet cheesecloth on top of the knitted surface and touching it lightly with a dry iron. Lift and set down the iron gently; do not use a pushing motion.

WET-BLOCKING

Soak in lukewarm water until saturated. Gently squeeze out much of the water (do not wring) and lay flat on a clean, dry towel or mesh drying rack; shape to measurements and leave until completely dry.

Resources

Yarn Sources

Special thanks to the following companies for their contributions of yarn for this book.

BERROCO
berroco.com
Modern Cotton and Vintage

BLUE SKY FIBERS
blueskyfibers.com
Alpaca Silk, Metalico, and Royal

CARON
yarnspirations.com
Simply Soft

LION BRAND
lionbrand.com
Fisherman's Wool and Superwash Merino

LOUET
louet.com
Euroflax

MADELINETOSH
madelinetosh.com
Tosh Merino Light

MALABRIGO
malabrigoyarn.com
Merino Worsted

MANOS DEL URUGUAY
fairmountfibers.com
Fino

PATONS
yarnspirations.com
Silk Bamboo

QUINCE & CO.
quinceandco.com
Sparrow

SCHACHENMAYR
us.schachenmayr.com
Catania

SHIBUI
shibuiknits.com
Baby Alpaca

SPUD & CHLOE BY BLUE SKY FIBERS
blueskyfibers.com
Sweater

WILLOW YARNS
willowyarns.com
Attire Light

Metric Conversion Chart

To Convert	To	Multiply By
Inches	Centimeters	2.54
Centimeters	Inches	0.4
Feet	Centimeters	30.5
Centimeters	Feet	0.03
Yards	Meters	0.9
Meters	Yards	1.1

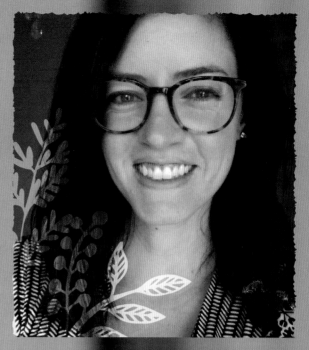

About the Author

Beth Nielsen is a fashion designer and yarn-craft addict, birth doula, stay-at-home-mom, and former musician living a modern bohemian lifestyle in Chicago, IL. She has contributed to Interweave Crochet and Crochet Today! magazines as well as 3 Skeins or Less: Quick Crocheted Accessories and It Girl Crochet, both by Sharon Zientara. Keep up with her at bethnielsen.com.

Acknowledgments

This book is dedicated to my babies, Malcolm and Thora, for through the writing process I gained a special understanding of the symbiosis of their happiness and mine. Also to my husband, Evan, who has always made my creative flourishing a priority in our life together. I'm so grateful.

Thank you also to Amy Bogert, Michelle Bredeson, and Christine Doyle who each talked me off the creative ledge more than once. They are gifted, encouraging people I'm blessed to work with.

To my technical editor, Daniela Nii, your precision and attention to detail are razor-sharp. My work is better for having been in your hands.

Thank you to Emily Reed and Deb Minnery, who lent their craftsmanship to sample samples.

Finally, to you, the reader. Whether you're just learning or you're a master, if them excites you, too, you're a part of my tribe. Thanks for holding this book in your hands.

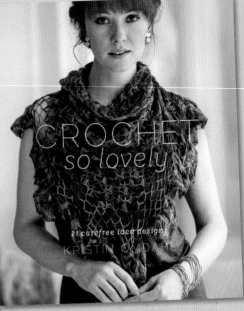
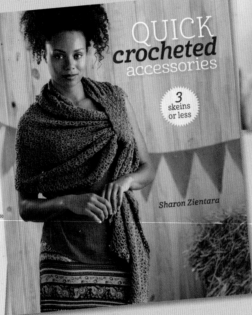
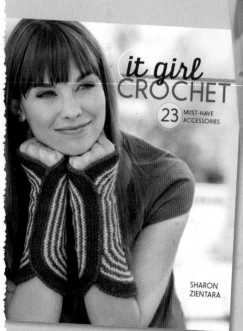
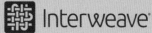